Our Ending Dark Age

Our Ending Dark Age

Stephen M. Barr

Writers Club Press
San Jose New York Lincoln Shanghai

Our Ending Dark Age

Writers Club Press
an imprint of iUniverse.com, Inc.

For information address:
iUniverse.com, Inc.
5220 S 16th, Ste. 200
Lincoln, NE 68512
www.iuniverse.com

ISBN: 0-595-14434-9

Printed in the United States of America

CHAPTER 1

Synthesis of Human Experience
The "Lessons of History"

How many times have we heard the old adage "History Repeats Itself"? It seems that when circumstances that seem to be out of our control arise, and we are able to key them to great milestones of the past, we foretell the outcome by saying history is repeating itself. Certainly in these last decades of the Twentieth Century great changes have been taking place that seem to cry out for this repetition. One of the favorites is the collapse of the Western Roman Empire that heralded the Dark Age.

Is there a basis for this? It does seem that our societies are becoming less governable. While many peoples of the more advanced countries—the "First World"—are still living a relatively decent, civilized existence, the evidence of worldwide chaos is increasing. Migrating peoples in ever growing numbers are looking for food, shelter, employment and safety—leaving areas of increasing economic and social deprivation and chronic warfare; increasing the numbers of people living in other countries as refugees. The result, along with the growth of home-grown barbarianism in the developed countries, is the deterioration of the very basic fabric—the unwritten

1

codes of human intercourse that are the basis for written law—that define our civilization.

And there is increasing evidence of a looming environmental crisis: The depletion of oceanic fisheries—the sea yielding about all it can, with the average available per person continuing to drop. The virtual extinction of increasing numbers of anadramous fish migrations; the breakneck harvesting of forests at rates far greater than their rates of restoration; especially the loss of tropical rain forests being exceeded by the loss of temperate forests extending far north of the equator; disappearing birds with 2/3 of all species on the decline and about 1000 threatened with extinction; grain stocks at their lowest levels ever—without any surpluses in many areas—as human populations continue to rise; destructive insects developing resistance to more and more poisons, with at least 17 species unaffected by any insecticide; increasing salinity of arable soils due to irrigation practices coupled with a high rate of topsoil loss worldwide. The nearing depletion of great aquifers and—already in some parts of the world—countries finding water to be more valuable than oil and willing to go to war over it; and lastly the sheer press of humanity on a finite world the results of a species that has overcome the natural controls on its numbers—disease and infant mortality—while not electing to voluntarily limit its size.

So with growing governmental chaos, brigandage, lawlessness, and increasing environmental problems, one could say that history is repeating itself and we are descending into a Dark Age. But we aren't, for we are still in the one that began with the collapse of Rome— though we are now living through its final stages. The reasons for this are complex, and to understand them we must analyze the historical record. But first we must digress. What is meant by historical record is to view history in its entirety—a synthesis, or if you will, a "unified" concept of history.

Albert Einstein and Stephen Hawking have brought physics to the point where we are on the verge of understanding a "unified" concept of the universe. Charles Darwin, evolution and a rapidly developing understanding of genetics and the genetic code are bringing us to an understanding of the biological interrelationships of all living things—a "unified" concept of life. As yet, however, we have not had a "unified" concept of history. To most history seems dry, or boring, sometimes arcane and usually irrelevant to what is happening "today". Yet the evidence for a "unified" concept of history is present—it has been growing as rapidly as that of physics and biology; for technological advances have allowed a more farreaching and detailed analysis of the historical and archaeological evidence.

Unfortunately, history is a vast and complex subject. It does not lend itself easily to the inductive methods that explain physics and biology. This complex size has reduced historians to try to find meanings, reasons, trends, etc; in areas of limited scope. They were not in error doing this—for their conclusions have been justified by their analysis of the evidence they used. A major locus of historical reference for many scenarios has been the "Dark Age". It has always been invoked as a giant step backward, a repressive evil that fell upon Europe (and other areas, for all civilizations have had dark ages) because of various erroneous courses taken and/or from unavoidable conditions.

From this, the general consensus has become that the Dark Age began with the collapse of the Western Roman Empire during the last quarter of the fifth century CE. The several analyses about why this occurred have ranged from Gibbon's great complex scenario to H.J. Haskell's assertion that it became enervated from extensive socialistic economic programs. Others, like Wells and the Durants, claim that it was part of a natural process, having happened before—the barbarians are "always at the gates". Toynbee also was of this latter view, yet he went farther in asserting that there have been twenty civilizations in history that have collapsed—we are now living in the twenty first.

These historians and others have tried to derive a synthesis from the historical record, a "meaning" or "philosophy"—a unified theory—of history. The Durants, in fact, titled their synthesis "The Lessons of History", implying the past can indicate future direction in order to prevent chaos or another Dark Age. The lessons of history, however, cover not only the wide range of human experience, but more importantly the general trend of knowledge gain that marks the basic foundation of human experience throughout history. So this range of experience includes knowledge of climate, geography, economics, philosophy, religion, politics and the newest of sciences that is providing the link among all, psychology. Viewing history this way reveals how the trends and attitudes mankind has experienced have shaped each other while they influenced the very tides of civilization as they rose and fell among nations. As if societies are species experimenting with forms conceived to be the most capable, there has arisen throughout the centuries various governmental forms, economic systems and societal structures.

Regardless of the forms in which these societies were cast—democratic, theocratic, monarchial, capitalistic, militaristic, piratical, etc.—the concept of "civilization" within each is subjective. If the term "civilization" is defined as "proper behavior" or what is normal, then this subjectivity becomes apparent. The ancient Greeks thought themselves civilized while those that didn't share their ways—other peoples—were barbarians. For centuries, the Chinese considered themselves inhabitants of the "Middle Kingdom", the only civilized nation lying between heaven and the rest of humanity. Every people has at one time considered themselves the "chosen of God", having been placed in a location created by the very deity of whom they are the favorites. There are far too many of these stories to even begin to catalogue here, and that is not the purpose of this work. Rather, we should recognize that the people and nations of every continent has entertained stories such as this. The remarkable trait would be how basically similar they all are. Furthermore, with something so basic as religious stories being so similar, we can look beyond and ask the question are "civilizations" **really** separate?

Piecing together mankind's history within the purview of recent knowledge—psychological, anthropological, genetic, archaeological, etc.—shows us that civilizations have never really been separate. Since mankind first emerged as a tool using/making being, his advancement—his accumulation of knowledge—has been fairly steady, exhibiting an almost universal character. From its earliest days where the differences we like to characterize as social were developing as man was coping with and adapting to the fluctuations of the Ice Ages, the widespread universality of Stone Age culture attested to more than wide-ranging cultural contacts. The local differences that were superimposed upon this ancient culture were the results of satisfying local needs. These differences varied by region, and there were local differences within a region.

Nevertheless, though at different times, the general trend of development followed a similar path. Along with the development of local cultures—soon to become identified as tribal—and along with the development of regional cultures—soon to become identified as national—the large area-wide cultures developed in a fairly regular manner with fairly similar characteristics.

The regional and local differences that characterized prehistoric cultures were not caused by any differences or deficiencies among human tribes. They were direct results of differences in environment that occurred wherever a certain tribe chose to center their activities. Before the days of agriculture, man lived as hunter-gatherers; those tribes whose environment was rich in game and plant foods, weren't required to range very far to live year around. The more meager was food availability, the wider ranging the more "nomadic"—they had to be in order to live year around. These environmental differences—and the living requirements they imposed—also affected religious thought.

As soon as man began a tool industry he separated himself from Nature. The very act of manufacturing tools meant that his natural world became alien, something that made his life difficult. Tools were a means of alleviating the difficulty. But man's society is more than just a coordinated group of a certain species. The moment he decided to exist "ex-Natura" necessitated the development of a concurrent reality that gave him meaning and substance; something that enabled him to be on his own. This of course is his group conscience, his "community spirit"; his spirituality. This spirituality has been a fairly constant factor throughout all members of our species. It basically is the innate assurance that we will recognize each other as fellow human beings, no matter what accretions of prejudice later societies impose upon us. This assurance is universal, so as prehistoric civilizations developed in a fairly universal fashion, so did man's spiritual sophistication.

This universality of consciousness, or spirituality, is what carried mankind's prehistoric, and later historic, progress along on a fairly uniform basis. Although we don't have any factual evidence, we have surmised from archaeological evidence and anthropological studies that animism was most probably the first recognizable religious system devised. It enabled man to explain the reasons for events and circumstances that were becoming less obvious as his civilization evolved—and his separation from nature increased. There were local differences of conception of the animistic spirits, yet their general development was fairly uniform world wide. Environmental differences affected the maturation of animism. Those areas in which there was a bountiful availability of food and shelter found mankind's animistic conceptualization of the world around him served him quite well. Where life was more difficult, the spirits were less benign, more demanding—their propitiation demanded a very close adherence to exacting ritual. The impetus for civilization—that is; becoming civilized—was effected by the same forces. So from the earliest days there was a symbiosis between the environmental pressures that drove mankind to advancement, and the religious thought that was part of it. Those areas where living off the environment was easy, there was no drive to civilize, nor was it necessary to develop a more complex, demanding religion: Civilization in these area was slow in coming, in fact some have remained "primitive" to this day. Since living within their environment was not difficult, there was no need for a strict religious conceptualization of the world—no need to remind mankind of the harshness of existence and therefore no need for a demanding god with an exacting code of laws to help him in navigating through the vicissitudes of nature.

Those areas where living conditions were made difficult with annual river floodings, decided changes in the seasonal environment, or other such phenomena, forced mankind to follow a more rigorous life. Crops had to be stored, waterworks had to be built, manufacturing of various items had to be developed, and trade for those items unavailable for use was developed. All of this took a level of organization that was far beyond the primitive society; the individuals of society had to transform from generalists into specialists. Unlike the primitive society wherein the community bond provided a foundation for government, the more complex society of specialists required another group of specialists whose task it was to provide government; to maintain an organization among the tasks so that an overall view of the life of society is not lost.

Religion too, became more strict. As mankind's societies developed with greater numbers of more specialized tasks, there had to be developed a system of spirituality that maintained a sense of unity—of similarity or sameness—among all members. So religion had to become arcane; it had to require some effort to partake of its beneficence— more than just "living with" the spirituality of animism—thus was it able, by demanding adherence to its rules and rituals, to maintain that cohesiveness of spirit that was farther lost as mankind, in developing civilization, became even more divorced from Nature.

But the history of civilization, of religion and their interrelationship is an old story traversed by many historians. There is no need here to become bogged down in details, or recap all the nuances that characterized historical/religious development. What is more important is to realize the sameness, the uncanny similarity of ideas and conceptualizations of civilization and religion that characterized the rise of mankind. The only separate line of development took place in the Western Hemisphere, which was populated during the last ice age. After the ice receded, society evolved much like Darwin's finches, completely separated from the mainstream of humanity. Yet their reaction to the superior technological development of Europe that ushered in the beginning of "Modern History" was the same as the rest of the non-European world; quick acceptance of physical factors—the technology that made life easier—but a much slower assimilation of intellectual factors. Many of today's problems can be traced to this physical-intellectual dichotomy, a dichotomy that lies at the root of the continuing Dark Age.

Mankind has always desired to exist within a world state, yet the very process of expanding to create such a state brought exposure to new ideas, different cultures of different conceptualizations which sowed the seeds of dissolution. This dissolution has become called a "Dark Age" but should really be called an "Age of Adjustment". With the intrusion of new cultural mores, conceptualizations, religious ideas, etc; the nation must wrestle with sorting out the differing—at times conflicting—ideas so as to reach a consensus. Once this is done, rebuilding civilization again begins.

To historians this is an old story; each time a state has encompassed the "world", that world became much larger. While increasing the world state's range of awareness, and bringing upon it the very influences of destruction, however, there seems to occur a great flourish of intellectual activity before the historical "end".

When the Chow took over China's government, an era of expansion greater than that of the Shang began. Contacts of greater intimacy occurred with the Hsuing-nu to the north, Yueh-chih to the west and the Min in the south. As foreign political factions, business aims and cultural attitudes played to the political differences among the states, these differences became accentuated. These rivalries rose to such a level that the "Age of Contending States" began—the beginning of the end of the Chow dynasty. There was, however, a great flourishing of art, literature and technology; China's famous Golden Age of Philosophy represented by Confucius, Mencius and others.

This was repeated with the Han dynasty extending China's rule to Afghanistan and Vietnam. Again the state was exposed to numerous cultural influences that were manifested in political rivalries of greater rancor. China's era of the Sixteen Kingdoms began. But since the world to which China had become exposed was so large and wide ranging, reestablishment of a new society wasn't as easy as before—after the period of 16 Kingdoms, a long period of North—South division of several dynasties each limped along until all was conquered by the Mongols.

Overcoming many of the parochial rivalries about the Indian subcontinent, Mahapadma Nanda managed to establish the first Indian unified state. Yet by the time Chandragupta took over his mismanagement, India had already been assailed by both Persians and Siberian tribes fleeing the Chinese. Now Alexander and the Greeks entered the picture; India had been subjected to so many religious and cultural ideas imported from a world suddenly quite vast, that the end came within a few generations of Gupta rule.

The old "worlds" of the Akkadians, Sumerians, Assyrians and Hittites remained moribund after Egypt announced her end in the El Amara correspondence. Each of these "worlds" had arisen, were influenced by a wider world that brought their demise, and awaited their fate at the hands of the Persians. With the Persians came Indian and Chinese ideas and influences, only to be outdone by Alexander and the Greeks. Probably one of the richest eras in human history was the result—the Hellenistic era that spread from northern India to northern Africa, across Greece and into Italy and south-eastern Europe. As Alexander's empire broke up, and political rivalries rose to the fore—some of the world's greatest literature was created; great philosophical treatises were written and early scientific suppositions were made. The world was indeed quite a large, wide-ranging place to contemplate. The fractiousness into which it had descended awaited a new, greater, government that would again bring mankind under the umbrella of a "world state".

That government, waiting in the wings, was of course Rome. The growth of Rome into history's most renown "world state" was paralleled by those of the Han and Guptas. Knowledge of a greater world was spreading, as commercial contacts among these three worlds existed across the central Asian trade routes and the Roman trading ports in India that also hosted Chinese trading missions. As if in anticipation of the new mind-set necessary for assimilating this larger world concept, this era also saw the rise of new one-god-one-world religions; Buddhism, then Christianity and finally Mohammedanism, all in the span of a millennium. But then these religions were already playing to a world quickly sinking into chaos: Buddhism arose in an India racked by Aryan tribal dissensions, severely weakened after the great Mahabharata War, awaiting the intrusion of a greater world by the Persians and Greeks. Christianity arose in the political chaos of post-Alexandrian Hellenism just before Roman hegemony. Mohammedanism arose in reaction to the political, and especially Christian, confusion that continued after the fall of Rome.

But the evolution of individual thought that eventually coincides into acceptance of a "world state" is a long and chaotic process. That Europe and western Asia had broken up into so many small governmental regions made this process extremely difficult. Religion didn't help either; Christianity was of itself racked by dissension over its nature, its relationship to the individual, and how much it was to be involved in political affairs. And there were attempts to restore the Pax Romana of old—the Holy Roman empire, the British Empire, the Napoleonic Empire, the League of Nations, the Third Reich and now the United Nations and the European Economic Community.

But within this millennia and a half, the many individuals that make up mankind's "state of mind", those overt expressions of the universal subconscious have yet to achieve consensus. For every attempt at unity, the world became larger and more complex—upsetting nascent trends toward unity and peace. The West's opening up of Japan brought a greater world to that closed society, upsetting the established order; a struggle among royalty, tribal chieftans and the peasantry began, resulting in the great expansion that precipitated, in part, World War II. The West intruded into China—another closed society—likewise destroying a fairly unified society since the Yuan dynasty that was saved from complete dissolution only by Mao Tse Tung.

These, however—China, Japan, the Holy Roman Empire, etc.—are only bumps in long overall process of "Dark Age" readjustment. The collapse of Rome, the Guptas and the Han all occurred within a short span of time, resulting in a worldwide spread of chaos above which we have yet to rise. Religio-political wars were—and in some areas still are—a common state of society. As people struggle with establishing communities, to find their common grounds of coexistence, government was left to the privileged in order to determine nationhood and its character.

In Europe these battles were most intense—and complicated. The fight for political definition was highly influenced by the church which—carrying on its legacy of having been the sole organization of governmental scope after Rome's collapse—did not want to have its primacy eroded. This played out in not only contests over the scope of church authority in relationship to secular authority but also in political maneuvering within international relationships that such claimed clerical authority could be used as a means of persuasion, factional support, or to justify disobedience even to a justification for regicide. But Rome's influence did not completely disappear. There was a residue of Roman law present in those areas covered by the old empire. Unlike oriental kings whose rule by "divine right" was uncontrolled (except by extreme popular disapproval which usually resulted in assassination), European kings were limited by dependence on their councils—later parliaments—that controlled purse strings. Costs of political acts had to be taken into account—how much taxation were the people willing to bear. Unlike major oriental kingdoms that relied largely on conquest to control trade routes so that their acquisition of material was assured, highly factioned Europe had to depend on diplomacy, economic health and popular support for survival.

These political machinations demanded success in orchestrating politics, church, culture, economy and balancing them within a framework of international relationships. It didn't take long for a more comprehensive "world view" to begin to predominate. While Henry I had to play balance of power politics among Ireland, Scotland and France, with Henry V, these same rivalries had expanded to include the Dutch and, with the introduction of gunpowder, an added complication of maintaining trade relations to assure a supply of ammunition. By Elizabeth I's rule, all of Europe had become involved, very similar to China's "Age of Contending States", which, like China, gave rise to the great cultural fluorescence of the Renaissance—Europe's greatest period of art, music, architecture, literature and philosophy that lasted well into the 19th century.

Europe, however, was assailed by a new type of development that challenged self-perceptions and caused an almost continuous need for "readjustment"; science and technology. Emerging slowly at first, their cumulative buildup of knowledge continually upset society. A status quo existence became impossible as the results of scientific and technological development demanded greater interdependency among the countries of an expanding world. Something as simple as gunpowder required secure means to acquire sulphur and nitrates, not available in every country. While the iron ore trade had been in existence a long time, development of iron cannon with its more complicated accompanying equipment, brought about quite an increase, requiring an even greater reliance on trade routes, better ships and international relationships. With trade comes ideas, values and a host of other ways people deal with life, upsetting any chance of a society becoming set in any certain "status quo".

The spread of Mohammedanism with eruptive speed from the Hindu Kush across northern Africa was a jolt to Europe in the process of trying to establish its world view within the widening experiences of expanding world trade. The Moslems cut off many established trade routes—the result; the Crusades to regain access to former markets, the sailings under Prince Henry to circumvent the Moslem world, and the daring exploit of Columbus to avoid the Moslems altogether. Suddenly in the span of a mere 500 years a vast, very complex, world was brought into view. Whole systems of society, religious observance, cultural attributes, mores, science and technology, architecture and governmental/legal practices were both brought home to Europe and exposed one region to another. Within this half-millennium European governments matured into fairly efficient mechanisms (when in the hands of capable monarchs). Their adherence in a majority of times to law, fiscal responsibility and care for the wellbeing of the commons, created a preindustrial dynamism that carried their European balance of power international politics beyond Europe and around the world. Never since the Alexandrian-Roman expansion had there been such a profound counter-influencing of cultures. Now it was a precursor of being global, setting mankind out on a path of complexity that multiplied the factors of social disruption beyond anything heretofore seen. The quest for free trade routes and the establishment of trade depots ("factories") quickly became enmeshed in the political chess-game among the dominant European powers—Portugal, Spain, France, England and the Dutch. Trade depots became bases for colonial empires; empires seen as the means to guarantee markets and raw materials for emerging industrialization, but also used in flanking moves to out maneuver one or another power so as not to have this economic establishment threatened. So the British-French conflicts in Africa and Asia; British, French, Russian then also United States conflicts in North America (in which the indigenous peoples became unwilling pawns).

As the Moslem tide, European expansionism and the Renaissance quickly tumbled in on one another, many cried out for stability. The Counterreformation was one of these movements, but it too was soon lost in the inexorable tide of European dominated readjustment: The sheer complexity of a multi-faceted world made imposition of any rational order at that time an impossibility. Added to this mix was the introduction of further complexity—the printing press and the beginning of true scientific method. As presses grew in numbers and produced an ever increasing amount of information, reactions by greater numbers of people to what was going on around them translated into even more political and social turmoil. But it was the rise of scientific method that produced the most disruptive influences of all on human society—its development continues to this day while the human reaction has been one of continued social unrest and warfare. While the press opened greater numbers of minds to the wider vistas of world knowledge, the establishment was upset by this challenge to their power of "spin control". This establishment was, however, the same as it had been for all of man's history heretofore; agriculturally based. Despite the disruptive forces that an expanding nation/state brings upon itself, there was an attempt to maintain a semblance of order as the government tried to coordinate policy with an established religion. In an agricultural society, policy and revenue are dependent on successful planting and harvesting seasons. The regularity (hopefully) of these seasons fit well with the regularity of life advocated by the established religions. Religions which preached regularity in reaction to themselves having been founded in times of turmoil.

It was the rise of scientific method, however, quickly followed by industrialization that provided for the most thoroughgoing disruption of human society at that time. New centers of economic power arose, and great movements of people-workers—began. Government policies became far more complex; from new social problems from great numbers of peoples no longer self-sufficient on farms to involved international problems of raw materials acquisition and trade route security. These problems accompanied the European juggernaut as it swept around the world with its superior industrializing economy—and as other nations found that their existence was best assured by adapting a similar economy. It was like these countries were struck by a thunderbolt; old societies long inured to an agriculturally based economy memorialized by an established religion had their social structure that was geared to this organization completely disrupted.

But the old order dies hard. The structure of kings and courts—the government of a religio-agricultural society—saw its greatest defeat during World War I. Meanwhile, the rise of industrialization was accompanied by two factors, the penultimate stages before the end of our long, long Dark Age. First is the rapidly increasing development of technology, which from the American Civil War on engendered warfare practices of mass destruction and killing. Conflicts became ever more bloody, many with an undercurrent of genocidal "justification". Second is the rise of democracy, dreams of people given a sense of selfsufficiency by an industrial economy that allows greater individual freedoms (no longer "tied to the Earth" and religion). Yet democracy is an ending stage of mankind becoming ever more finely divided as the chaos of the end of our dark age nears. The coalescence of many states into larger nations—United States, India, China, USSR, Great Britain, Spain, France, Germany, and others—has been called "the rise of Nation States", but they are bumps in the long process in mankind's quest for unity, for coalescence. These "nation states", however, have been plagued by being "established" in a world plagued by disruption of the status quo: They have been increasingly racked by the centrifugal forces of separatism.

A new understanding of the world's economy and its consequent necessary social structure, however, has emerged in recent years. Since the economic disruption of the Napoleonic wars, a growing number of national leaders have been realizing the increasing economic interdependency of peoples. Brought into sharper focus with the American Civil War and the Franco-Prussian war, full impact of what a fully integrated world portends was first realized by early 20th century presidents of the United States. Thereafter the necessity for establishing a humanity that lives within a worldwide "state" was thrust upon all nations by World War I and its more comprehensive after-result, World War II. Many world leaders forsaw the inevitability of worldwide political and economic integration. Yet again, the old orders die hard; resistance to the League of Nations (the United States senate refused to join) brought about its collapse at the beginning of World War II. A more comprehensive organization was created with the United Nations, yet there is still very much resistance to giving it the supranational authority it needs. Yet the United Nations provided a forum that, for the first time in history, displayed national aspirations, political intrigues and cultural biasness for all the world to see, analyze and judge. There was an attempt to regularize the world's economic order by establishing various economic treaty relationships and funding programs (such as the Bretton Wood's Conference and the World Bank). The impact on the "status quo" these programs had was significant, yet not as thoroughgoing as the technological advancements of the last several decades.

Communication satellites and computer networks have brought instant accessibility of information from anywhere in the world to anyone capable of acquiring it. People and businesses are connecting globally, surpassing the abilities of governments to control this rising tide of information. More and more, borders of our "nation states" are becoming less important as this increasing tide of information availability and access sweeps around the world. Religious and social customs everywhere are being scrutinized, analyzed and judged. Governments are grappling with economic problems that are no longer controlled by themselves, a situation not understood by most of their citizens. The press of human numbers and its environmental impact is no longer local, or national—but realization of global effects are becoming more widely recognized. One manifestation of these problems is a dawn of a new "age of migrations" as more and more people are displaced by nations and regions increasingly less able to feed, employ, house and minister their burgeoning population. From the establishment of the United Nations to communication satellite technology, a new "world state" has been thrust upon humanity. The disruption of family values—indeed, the very definition of "family" itself—morals, attitudes, religious stances and justifications, economic and political reasoning, are all being subjected to a thorough-going analysis. Never before have the foundations of human existence been shaken so thoroughly to their core as they are today. And finally, the significance of modern civilization is that it is completely foreign to the natural rhythms of mankind's evolved "normalcy". Up until recently, the first million or so years of human existence has been shaped by the environment in which mankind existed. His reaction to it, and how he adapted to it, shaped every facet of culture, both prehistoric and historic: Mankind's religions, family structure, interpersonal relationships, societal mores and economic structures have all evolved in response, and therefore in relation to, this environment. The twentieth century, however, was the beginning of a new era in which mankind achieved the ability not only to alter (which he has always been able to do) but to control his alterations of his environment. Exercising this control is eliminating our need to be referenced to the world around us. Without this reference, mankind's society is being cast adrift. It is becoming more unsettled as we search for a new reference datum upon which to shape our future society. Until a great world-wide consensus is reached on this plethora of problems—indeed even our very root basics of family, morals, religion and community—it is then that our long Dark Age travail will come to an end.

CHAPTER 2

Man: What, How, Why and Who?

Before we can understand the mechanism that drives the evolution of Man's history along with its cyclic rises and falls, we must understand the nature of man himself. While there is much speculation and theorizing about how life began—that is, the cause for the appearance of living molecules—that story lies within the continuing work of science. Our concern here is with the first living beings—called organisms of the Archeozoic Age—and their consequent specialized development.

But first we must digress into considering the concept of evolution of which mankind has been both a part and a product. Many detractors discount evolution because of the absence of evidence of intermediate forms; those forms that would have shown transition steps between the phyla. This argument, however, merely begs the question, completely avoiding gains in genetic knowledge that has become a powerful guide to the evolutionary process. It has now become common knowledge that genotypes show a progressive interconnected development when they're followed along the phyla. The general similarity of DNA molecules among the various phyla shows close connection among them and demonstrates that minor genetic changes (mutations) can create significant physical changes that preclude the existence of large populations of "intermediate forms". More exacting is the existence of mitochondrial DNA, a sort of "constancy factor" that regulates rate of evolutionary change and prevents wide divergence within a species if populations are widely scattered. Mitochondrial DNA is perhaps the key in the evolutionary process. Its very slow change through the millennia parallels the slow change within a species' evolution. A most demonstrative example is with mankind's evolution—using computer simulations of changes that would normally occur within the molecular biological structure of mitochondrial DNA, a measure of rate of change for the human species can be ascertained. The anthropological record of human evolution that has been determined recently matches the human record.

There are, however, problems with evolution that are not ones of evidence but of perspective. One is that man cannot imagine the world without himself in it—a world teeming with life. A world in which predation is only from need. There is an absence of territorial exclusivity, that is, environments were by and large shared by a great many species. There was not the exclusion—or attempt to—of other species as man does. This exclusivity began far back into prehistory, so when concepts of language and philosophical reasoning arose, exclusivity had become so "natural" that a concept of sharing the earth had a completely different meaning. So the great complex milieu of many species sharing an environment—conditions under which evolution worked its way—has not been a common reference for humanity.

A second problem is that of the missing so-called "intermediate" forms. This is coupled with mankind's inability to **really** comprehend the vast amounts of time we are dealing with. Considering the numbers of individuals of each species within the great complex milieu, the fossil record we have is a minuscule sample of the totality. Keep in mind that fossils are the record of the very successful forms: Those forms that in evolving to a position in which there was relative security of their existence, reproduced and continued over a very long period of time. The more abundant the remains and so the greater possibility for fossilization. Intermediate forms would not be competently favored, and so would not have a long time of existence. This results in an extreme paucity of fossilized remains which even by the luck of favorable geologic activity and a fossil hunter's skill, may never be found.

Lastly is the question "why?". Indeed, why evolution at all? What reason would there be for life to develop beyond the Archeozoic level of single-celled forms. Consider that as single cell forms, their life was their own—their own "being" so to speak. To become a multi-cellular being required the sacrifice of giving up some independence to join a cooperative. But first there had to be a way for each of the cells in a cooperative to know their function and/or how they relate to their companions. With the development of chromosomal trait recording, this became possible. Chromosomes appeared about 1 1/4 billion years ago, a considerable time after the appearance of the first life forms about 4 1/2 billion years ago. How chromosomes came to be developed in cells is a question we may never answer. But why is obvious—to carry traits on from generation to generation and maintain the cooperative organization. One could wonder if there are small changes a cell or simple organization of cells could initiate within themselves to better meet changing conditions. This is not to say that Lamarkianism is a factor in evolution, but simple organisms have an amount of control over acceptance or rejection of mutations that we higher beings cannot imagine. This process takes place among the higher beings, but since our "selves" are so remote from our cellular "roots", we are totally unaware of its presence. So we must look at our evolution, and perhaps the significance of our cellular roots will become apparent.

A secondary question to "why evolution?" is "why **not** evolution?". That is, why did some forms evolve while others apparently did not? Evolution is the acceptance of random change insofar as it enables a species to better cope with its environmental circumstances. If those circumstances change, and beneficial mutations occur along with these changes, then that species will change to retain its best "fit" with the new environment. But if mutations do not occur with environmental change, then a being's "will to live" (more about this below) drives it to adapt to the new conditions. In this way, may species are able to adjust in order to live many diverse ecological relationships. The "need" to alter, to develop into a new species becomes unnecessary, and the forces of extinction are thwarted.

While there is still much speculation and theorizing about how life began—that is, the cause for the appearance of living molecules—that story lies within the continuing work of science. Our concern here is with the first living beings—the single celled organisms of the Archeozoic Age—and their consequent specialized development.

The first cells were very simple affairs; life was easy floating in the mineral rich soup that was the oceans of aeons ago. As they basked in sunlight living in this soup, food that was this soup, was so plentiful that there was no need for competition. Eventually, however, their numbers became so great that this ease of food availability began to lessen. A need for competitive stature arose as the cells increasingly had to scrabble for their food. Coupled with this new competitiveness was the randomness of the results of reproduction. Before the advent of chromosomal trait transfer, the results of cell division was unpredictable, with results ranging from two cells the same as their parent to one cell perhaps like the parent and one without enough ingredients with which to even stay alive. Those with chloroplasts were the same; there may be two with chloroplasts or one with and one without. This problem of non-uniform consistency in reproduction was solved with the introduction of chromosomal trait transfer. The mechanism for evolutionary process was now in place, as mutations were minimized by genetic change eliminating the gross physical changes that occurred before. But genetic trait transfer forced life into two camps: Those with chloroplasts continued to live off of sunlight and suspended minerals; those without were forced to become predators. The rapid reproduction—sort of like yeast budding—of the old days no longer could occur. Chromosomal reproduction was slower, more methodical—and subjected the dividing cell to attack during division. So competition for food was beset by another factor, defense against predators. With chromosomal genetic transfer, rapid reproduction (or as rapid as possible) wasn't always the best defense. In time, the simplest of defense measures was organization: Cells would join together in cooperative groups; the first steps of a more complex evolution.

We are not concerned here with the why or how of evolution. What is important to understand, however, is the development of organization; of cellular specialization that became more stringent as life developed in greater complexity. So cooperative groups were of a very simple nature; no specialization was required but a uniformity of shape was accepted. Since life began in the sea, as long as each cell was touched by water, each had access to food. Those that had chlorophyll were lucky, for sun-light and water (with its load of minerals) were utilized to manufacture food. Those without chlorophyll had to acquire food either by being predators or eating the chlorophyllites—the plants. We aren't concerned here with plant evolution, even though in their earlier stages, organization was somewhat similar to animals.

As we move through the phyla in developmental order—that is, in the order of animal life's evolution—we see cell groups coping with more complicated demands of organization. Coupled with the necessity to maintain defense against predators, the result has given the world its great variety of life, both extinct and extant.

So even if our single string of cells grouped together with other strings and formed a tube, each cell would still have access to the sea. Perhaps the inner cells would have cilia to increase water flow through the tube giving inner cells both greater access to seaborn nutrients and an adequate means to expel waste. This is exactly how sponges work. They are the highest form of life that is made up of cooperating cells. Every cell in a sponge has access to the sea; many have cilia to pump water through their sometimes complicated form.

Following evolution through the phyla, we can speculate as to the why of increasing complexity of life forms. But that is another well traversed story. Our concern here is the increasing complexity of each organism as various cells agree to carry out more specialized tasks. Tubular systems soon became closed bodies as in the polyps in which

seawater can still reach all cells through a mouth of specialized sphinc-
ter cells that also serves to expel waste. Some cells, as in jellyfish, may
serve as eyes—both for defense and food spotting—while there is a
joint cooperation in moving the animal by all cells. Soon, however,
joint cooperation became less tenable as the demands for more coordinated and rapid movement in defense and acquisition of food
required a more sophisticated development. More and more, cells
became increasingly specialized so that the evolving organism could
more adequately meet these demands.

So hollow bodies gave way to solid bodies. Some cells became mus-
cles that moved the body. Other cells specialized in food handling,
replacing a hollow body with an alimentary system. Eyes became
more sophisticated, developing from light sensitive cells to systems of
greater complexity in which greater detail could be discerned. Some
outer cells became a defensive bulwark; a layer of hardened covering
that reduced the probability of an organism being penetrated by some
form of predator. These specializing cells, as they became buried
deeper in bodies of a more substantial makeup—and even those serving as eyes and skin—no longer had access to the sea. Food and
oxygen had to be brought to them, while their waste products had to
be taken away. Further specialization occurred as cells formed vessels
to circulate seawater (or a sea-water type substance—blood) to them,
with cells within this fluid serving as bearers. With increasing complexity, a central pumping plant had to be set up—a heart—to move
the fluid through the vessel system, itself of growing complexity.
Other cells had to specialize as gills in extracting oxygen from seawater for transport throughout the system.

With this rapidly increasing complexity, a most important factor
concurrently developed. So that different groups of cells performing
different specialized tasks didn't become lost in performing their tasks,
a system had to be established that enabled the cells to maintain their
awareness that this complex organism of which they are part has
evolved solely as a vehicle for maximizing their longevity. A means had
to be established that maintained each cell's worth in its participation

within living organisms of increasing complexity as evolution pro-gressed. With more explicit specialization in which cells could lose their reason for existence, the means derived to maintain their intercon-nectedness was the development of nerves. That is, some cells became specialists in communication, providing a network by which a more complex organism could enjoy the same coordination of activity enjoyed by simpler beings. Moving through the phyla, however, we find beings comprised of aggregates of more narrowly defined tasks. Something more than a "time share" network of nerves had to begin coordinating the many tasks. A brain was developed as a Central Processing Unit that took over this function.

Although each cell's range of "life experience" narrowed as task specializations became more numerous, the being as a whole carries a response reflex to environmental changes that is a cumulative record of each cell from their ancient single-cell days. As beings were com-prised of vast numbers of cells divided into greater numbers of specialized tasks, survival depended upon reacting faster than waiting for reaction input from all cells. The brain, therefore, enabled this being that is an organization of a vast number of cells to react quickly to environmental events. Inotherwords, the brain, as "central process-ing unit", is able to coordinate the reflexual reactions of the vast number of cells it heads into a general direction where the resultant context is considered an instinctual operation.

As evolution progressed, two things occurred. The brain itself spe-cialized; part becoming an "engineering deck" to handle daily operation of repetitivetasks. Another part became a "management deck" to handle instinctual operations. This management was more than just handling instinct, there was some reasoning capability. Small at first, but as evolution progressed and coordinated with the second development—a change from exoskeleton and armor plate to interior skeleton with complex muscular development and pliable skin cover-ings—reasoning ability advanced, integrating with instinct until purely instinctual reactions became minimal. This is not to say all acts are by reason. With flexible interior skeletons, soft sensitive body coverings and highly developed sense preceptors, the reactions that would normally be instinctual—the "cellular response"—was now analyzed within a wider environmental realm as to its feasibility. With the evolution of mankind, a dimension of the brain's "management deck" expanded to capabilities far beyond anything seen before. Reasoning advanced beyond being applied for the moment, but was being utilized in the theoretical. Learning became much more rapid. Now consideration is given to what "might happen", and what would be a proper response. And this response could be contrary to an instinctual response. The individual "self" of the human individual emerged as mankind became more and more a species of his own creation. Instead of theorizing how he would react in certain situations, he set about changing the environment in order to direct the course of events to **insure** that his theorized reactions would be correct. The human individual became more pronounced, for reactions to anticipated and (theorized) unanticipated events became a group function. How he was to act and react became a function of being schooled by his group. Yet genetics has a say in this also: While all members of society receive the same perceptions through fairly similar senses, the pathways within the brain that are followed in order to associate ideas—make sense out of perceptions—is a function of construction by genetic plan.

So for the second time in Earth's history, the cell has triumphed in its struggle to gain security. By agreeing to differentiate into a highly organized complex mechanism, it has developed a structure that assured its greatest amount of security within the ecological niche into which it's organism evolved and within the standard Darwinian laws of existence. First to rise to the top of the heap were dinosaurs who were a triumph of security they ruled Earth for millions of years. Yet they declined, with the larger forms disappearing. Some say this was caused by a great cataclysmic collision of an asteroid with Earth. More than likely it was a combination of single cell/viral evolution—developing diseases that overcame many—and environmental changes to which the animals were unable to adapt.

Now mankind has risen to the top. This vast, highly complex organization of cells wherein many specialized tasks are being performed, all under the organizational aegis of the most highly developed brain Earth has yet seen, is no longer at the mercy of environmental change. At least not to the extent that he may become extinct. The cellular dream of aeons ago has finally been achieved; a being that is capable of an extremely variable defense. A being that is able to control—to varying extent—those forces that threaten its security.

What now becomes clear is the source of several attributes, some of which have seemed "natural" traits. The "Will to Live", exhibited by all living things, is merely the aggregate quest for security expressed by each cell in the organism—the whole point of the "why" of evolution as has been described. But mankind is a significant jump in the ongoing evolution of reasoning abilities beyond mere instinct, or at least "reasoned" or controlled instinct. This ability has forced mankind into a new plane of existence. He is no longer an "animal" in the sense that his evolution is controlled by chance, environmental change and the collective drive of cellular aims. Now his physical evolution has slowed, being replaced by social evolution; for the body politic—its cyclic evolution and its manifestations—now shape the parameters of his evolution.

The necessity of having a society that is rather unanimous in accord, hinges on the cooperation of individuals. And the more unanimous in accord, the more fit—more capable of maintaining itself—it is. This accord necessitates the cooperation of individuals, cooperation of many who share the "universal subconscious" yet may perceive the world around them in different individual—ways. So to have a competent society, there must be a fairly substantial number of its individuals exercising a fair amount of social accord.

But who, or what, is the "individual"? How did he become separate from his species, as opposed to those beings governed more by instinct? What is the "self"—who is the "I" that looks with these eyes and does not perceive others as I perceive myself? The "Individual" is a member of the human species with a brain that has grown far beyond regulating instinctual operations—it is the recipient of two forces. One it is the final repository of the body's aggregate cellular "will to live". The other is double pronged; the genetic randomness of laying out the brain's pathways by which sense input is analyzed, and how the association of ideas are carried out; and the effect society has on reforming or changing these pathways—this latter a function of the aggregate cellular drive for self-preservation; the "will to live".

The "will to live", of course, being the aggregate manifestation of each cell within our being's "will to live", is the triumph of that drive for security sought by life since the dawn of time. But the emergence of a highly developed brain in homo sapiens, along with the suppression of common subconscious—or instinctual—cooperation by individualism, has brought to bear upon mankind a new factor in the evolution of the species. Now intellectual competence has become the main factor deciding if the human animal is competent enough to survive. The quest for a great world state necessitates a premise consensus among humanity's teeming individuals. That we have been a long Dark Age—an Age of Adjustment—since the fall of Rome, Gupta and Han, is testament to these many individual's searching for that consensus. One of the most powerful forces that tries to forge the "will to live" into a consensus that can be accepted by everyone is religion. But even religion during the Dark Age is under attack. Its tenets, its veracity, indeed even its usefulness are being argued. The vast amount of change that has occurred over the last 1500 years of our history has shaken mankind's foundations of existence. Religion has become subject to individual interpretation, and so its ability to establish a consensus is gone. Religion does, however, play a part in society. What this part is, and how it effects the interrelationships among individuals and their "wills to live" must now be examined, so that we can move closer to understanding our great Dark Age and what must occur to rise out of it.

CHAPTER 3

God: Connection of Soul

In the last chapters mention was made of the "universal subconscious". It was also referred to as a kind of interconnected spirit that allowed members of a species to recognize each other as like members of that species. Modern mankind tries to identify this interconnectedness of ourselves with such terms as "spirit" or "soul". These terms, however, and others like them, are genera of religious reflection on mankind's "meaning". With the development of Homo sapiens sapiens' brain wherein the gauge of the species' most basic emotions—those of instinctive reactions—are the refinement of an aggregate of cellular survival techniques. We like to think that our higher emotions and actions/reactions are manifestations of our higher "being", our spiritual foundation or the orientation of our soul. But our emotions have developed from these basic instinctive survivalist reactions filtered through the change our evolutionary basis has undergone: That is, by graduating from an evolutionary orientations based on physical change to one of social change, our reactions and emotions have likewise altered to better integrate with this new condition.

And what a change! We experience more than those emotions based upon our natural roots—fear, peace, ease, satiety—we experience more highly developed emotions. Emotions that are so much a part of ourselves that our lives, so inextricably intertwined with our society, are not fully complete without their full play. So we cannot really know joy without knowing sadness. We cannot really know happiness without knowing tragedy. Nor love without hate. Nor trust without distrust. These are but the emotions of the individual, and at times of groups. But these evolve into more complex states that become so much a part of our evolving society that it cannot exist without them. For our society provides the basis for all or our emotions—the ones favored and those we'd rather avoid. But with the development of society, and as these simpler emotions became themselves intertwined within this complex structure, they mature into a greater complexity that provides the heart and soul of civilization. They become group, or communally, oriented, at times overriding the basic, simpler, emotions of the individual and oftentimes demanding a subservience to group expression so that the fabric of society isn't torn apart. Among these more complex group—or societal—emotions are compassion, empathy, charity, kindness, good will, justice—expressions of community that are the roots of what Rousseau called the "Social Contract" that raises us above barbarism.

Mankind, though, is not monolithic in nature. As we have seen in chapter 2, the complexity of the organism that resulted from security that drove some cellular beings to higher development, was further developed by endowing mankind with a more complex brain. This complex brain has given rise to individualism and the ability to interpret the world around each individual in terms relative to that individual. To most, this can be a very disconcerting state. So from the very beginning, when mankind perceived his "separation" from Nature, he strove for some unifying factor. For most of mankind's existence, his society—or "pre-society" relative to today's organizations—was that of the Hunter-Gatherer. The unifying factor here was animism in which the individual shared a spiritual existence with all parts of nature. Every plant, every animal, every human, indeed every mountain, river, lake, cloud, star, etc; even the sun and moon, contained a spirit that was part of an aggregate spiritual wholeness that embodied all of mankind's existence. This spiritual sharing provided both a foundation for existence and a sense of unity among individuals.

But as mankind developed civilization that was more sophisticated than his hunter-gatherer groups, need for a more overriding premise of unity became necessary. The knowledge of security from a passive acceptance of the world as is wouldn't work for differently organized societies. When trade networks, crop harvests, irrigation works and a host of other activities that depended upon regular results, became important, a certain measure of control over the environment became necessary. The passive animistic spirits needed to be given a measure of control—and they needed a form to which mankind could appeal in hopes of having this control guided in his favor. So along with the evolution of early civilization animistic spiritualism evolved into pantheism.

Now the world became virtually inanimate. There were many Gods that controlled both the natural acts of the world around us and also had a hand in influencing management of society. In addition, mankind had lost the sense of belonging he had when he shared with the animism of the natural world. This meant a loss of direction for natural acts were now seen in terms of benefit or harm. Passive acceptance had to be replaced by moral law and ethical considerations. Concepts that dictated the fabric of society integrated with the pantheon so that propitiation of the gods—living correctly—garnered the greatest benefit for society.

As we saw in chapter 1, however, when nations expanded where they began to abut each other and have intimate relationships there arose religious conflicts. The attributes of one pantheon did not exactly correspond to the attributes of another. The world was expanding and a foundation of morals and ethics had to be established that was region-wide. Deities could no longer take part in man's affairs, for this would mean that some could work at counterpurposes. This would not do; there had to be an overriding code that was applicable to all the various countries of the "world". So as we saw in chapter 1, in the millennium centered on the beginning of the common era (CE)—a time in which the nations of the world were recognizing a much greater world around them—there arose several overriding codes that are with us yet today. These of course are the "one world, one god" religions, the first being Buddhism and the last Mohammedanism. Now mankind was on his own, he no longer had as intimate a relationship with this god as he did with the pantheon. The world was run now the way god wished to run it. God no longer held the familiarity of human trials, tribulations and foibles that the pantheon shared with mankind. God was now aloof and dictated laws that mankind must obey to survive. Oh mankind could pray, offer supplication, hope to live by rules he studies assiduously in a holy book, and even in some cases sacrifice an animal, another human or a child. In the end, however, mankind had to accept how things turned out because, after all, they were "God's will".

Coupling this will of God with the corpus of laws governing human relationships that had evolved from the very primitive days of our hunter-gatherer society, a newer system came about. To reflect the more complex relationships that exist within mankind's agricultural societies of that millennium, these new codes of law were more sophisticated. They were written down, placed in "Holy Books" of unchallengeable authority, for the complex laws and moral dictums were "a priori" from God. Even though these laws had evolved parallel with the evolution of mankind's society, and their sophistication increased with the growing complexity of civilization, knowledge of the primitive roots of these codes was long forgotten. These roots were, of course, the natural low under which mankind lived "before civilization". What was needed was some sort of code of law that organized society in a way that reflected the new reality. So these laws were a priori, given by God, both because the roots were forgotten and this gave them a measure of authority.

To make all of this relative to the individual came under the purview of spiritualism. God may be remote, and his laws may be interpreted by clerics, but the direct connection was with the soul. Here then was an attribute of long forgotten primitive times that had remained and probably not changed much, although—since our natural connections have been lost—defining has become more difficult. As we have seen, we have been long separated from our natural roots, having lost almost all or our "natural knowledge" or direct "feel" for them. In the meantime, the development of language accompanied our search for ways to divine these roots. So we have come up with Spirit and Soul to both express our natural roots and the basic interconnectiveness of all humans. But being of language born ex-natura, these terms—these words—do not accurately define nor describe their concepts.

The soul merely orients the individual within the self that was discussed in chapter 2. This "I", this unique selfness for want of a more understandable concept than that of chapter 2 has become known as the spirit—the life force. More accurately, the Soul is our vital life principle of feeling, thought and action. It is our moral force, our force of feelings (emotions) and sentiments. The soul is incontrovertible, it is absolute. The soul is therefore that underlying life-force by which we recognize each other as members of the same species and is also thus the foundation of moral conduct: Members of the same species do not willingly or willfully harm or commit negative acts on other members.

The soul, then, is that part of the individual that connects each of us as members of one species; in essence the universal subconscious. This repository of a priori—born of basic respect of each member of a species for each other—moralism, is again trapped by the limitations of language that has evolved a natura. We do not have any words that accurately describe the soul in its natural characteristics. So by being unable to be accurately defined, the "Soul" has been pummeled by many and diverse attempts at definition. Attempts that have been made by various philosophies, be they religious or secular, yet have been so influenced by spirit that no irrefutability has occurred.

The Spirit is the manifestation of the soul in the expression of conscious life; it is the animator—the connection between body and soul. Spirit is that principle that can temper, adjust or even distort thought, feeling and action. Since the Spirit is the manifestation of the Soul, it is thus the basis of individual consciousness and conduct—it is the "I" of the self. It is subject to the evolutionary forces that direct society and civilization, and is influenced by historical trends. It can override the soul, thereby producing the great number of individuals that characterize human society. How an individual interrelates with his environment gives rise to his opinions. How these opinions, in their aggregate consensus, both influence and shape society and its civilization, have been major players in our long Dark Age. But we'll talk about opinion in the next chapter. The "oneness" of souls—that is, their intrinsic similarity—throughout our species, can be construed as a World Spirit. Here again is our problem with words, using spirit in the context of soul when above their differences were indicated. With the term World Spirit, however, is meant the "sense" of **all** souls in that they are quite similar. This may be construed a PANESSENCE, which more accurately describes the similarity of souls. Panessence is that intrinsic, indispensable property that serves and characterizes—or identifies—the species. It is that inherent, unchanging nature (soul) as distinguished from its existence (spirit).

There have been many attempts to define Panessence. These have ranged from various philosophical concepts, spiritualistic, occult to God. Closest perhaps was Schopenhauer's "World Spirit'" but this dealt with a future in which spirits were attenuated and the moral nature of human souls would take precedence. This is characteristic of our rise out of the Dark Age, and will be discussed in a later chapter. Now we must talk of Spirit and how both outside influences on it and its interpretation of the soul produces such wide ranging opinions. It is the interrelationships among opinions that are the grist of society and civilization; they produced the Dark Age and are the key to rising out of it.

CHAPTER 4

OPINION: Need for Simplicity

So far most of the foundation has been covered that will make under-standing emerging from our dark age a little easier. It is a complicated process for which the foregoing has tried to lay the groundwork. When the mechanisms of mankind's society are discussed in the next chapter, this groundwork will be an orientation aid in the direction of our historical progress. Realizing this progress needs understanding of the complex interrelationships within societies and their civiliza-tion. And to do this, we must first understand mankind himself.

So far the interrelationship of mankind's mental and physical facul-ties has been covered, as has the genesis of his gods, morality and the foundation of law. Yet, there is more: For with the examination of opin-ion, the very grist of civilization is reached. Opinion is the blood of society, indeed of civilization itself, and by the direction of its consen-sus, society's very orientation is aimed. Conversely, by its lack of direction (consensus) chaos results which means we must suffer a time of readjustment—that is, a "Dark Age".

As we have seen, the conflict between soul and spirit (as it relates to the state of society and civilization) gives rise to differing opinions. Without any sort of consensus, that is, without any general agreement among individuals, any kind of coexistence among them is impossible. Since all other species, especially those of a more congregative nature, live their agreement, which is simply their code of species recognition. Thus any individual separateness is tempered by the needs of the group. This is not to say that group members sacrifice—or deny themselves the carrying out of certain acts. Rather the "modus operandi" of each species is that mix of reason and code of instinctual activity with which they have evolved. There are no unnecessary or voluntary acts performed that lie outside those required for maintaining their existence; their maintenance of species competence within the parameters of their evolutionary niche.

With the emergence of mankind, his similar-to-the-other-species connections with the natural was not entirely lost. His first societies were of the hunter-gatherer type. They were egalitarian in which each member shared equal status within the scope of performing those acts that assure the survival of the group. These societies—for hunter-gatherers are types of societies—were ruled by the soul. The playout of life within the context of the laws of nature was normal: There was the acceptance of the vicissitudes of life not unlike the acceptance by other species. That is, the categorizing or conceptualization of occurrences within life as adverse or "vicissitudes" was unknown they were merely "life" as it is. Unique among mankind, however, was the rise of spirit in its domination of the soul. When did this happen? **When** was not a sudden occurrence but a slow evolution that was in and of itself the steady distancing of mankind from nature. When did a waist band used to hold tools and/or food become an object to be decorated, to express the individualism of the wearer? When did a rock heretofore used to kill game become a means of expressing one's dominance over another by becoming a weapon? When did a band used to tie back hair from the face become a piece for personal adornment?

These are indicative of Spirit beginning its ascendancy over Soul. Spirit, then, is the expression of mankind ex-natura, while Soul is, of course, **of** nature. Spirit, then, has no connection with the Panessence; no security of natural inclusion within a species group. No basis upon which to understand a reason for being, a justification for existence. So then Spirit is the inventor of God, the developer of religion. For these things provided the Spirit a reason for being and the justification for existence. As we have seen, however, environmental differences that characterized different locales have an effect on how an individual perceives and reacts to that locale. This is the realm of Spirit, for by not being of Nature, it is able to tailor one's response so that an occurrence's adverse effects are minimized and advantageous circumstances are capitalized upon.

So God becomes local because a deity must correlate with that society that holds it in esteem in order for that society to work. This is partly the reason why most colonialist intrusions throughout history have been so damaging: The overpowering of a local god by a foreign one destroys that society's ambient relationship with its local god that is in concert with the environment in which that society is set. But a local god did not suddenly appear as if by vote. It was itself a product of evolution—of the gradual aggregation of individual and family spiritual concepts interacting throughout society—a society itself that was in its early stages of development. All of this was spirit directed; the coalescence of individuals/families into societies was paralleled by the emergence of a spiritual consensus. Individual and early ("primitive"?) society's animism eventually could not serve a system in which egalitarianism was being replaced by specialization, ranking and management. As described in the first chapter, to cope with the growing complexity of society, animism gave way to the more comprehensive religious system of polytheism. This because early civilizations included more area—involved more than one clan—and so had to have a deity, or system of deities, that overrode the clan's animism yet did not offend (for the most part—for individualism never fully dies) the population's Spirit consensus.

As society develops, this symbiotic relationship with its religion—at first a survival mechanism within its environment—eventually gives it a "set". It develops a direction, or "track" that has become necessary by the governmental (including bureaucratic operation), social, economic and religious interrelationships by which it has matured. To change this track is difficult indeed, if not impossible. But change, as seen in the first chapter, has always been thrust upon mankind's organizations. And societies are much like humans, as they age they become "set in their ways"—they become inured to a certain mode of operation, a certain procedure that best serves their existence. So change becomes very difficult. Just as supersession of one god for another usually for the most part practically destroys a society, so does the imposition of a change that upsets the political, social and/or economic system.

Yet, as has been seen, change has always been thrust upon mankind's societies. In response there is always the drive for the soul-like existence of long ago, a return to "simpler times". Life based upon the soul is envisioned as simple (and so too religion which purports to be **of** soul) but the definition of this simplicity is spirit driven. And with the physical/genetic differences that define individualism, the spirit's expression of simplicity is manifested as pronouncements of opinions. Furthermore, a society's competence hinges on the amount of consensus among its individual members' opinions. For a society to work, the opinions of its members must be fairly similar; their consensus must include a great majority of the citizenry. As change intrudes, opinions are threatened. Challenged opinion gives rise to instability, for the competent power of the great consensus is lessened. Other consensi, heretofore holding only minor shares, gain wider recognition, along with new ones that have adopted a deducted opinion (pro or con) from the intrusive changes. The result is a society that seems chaotic and unstable, which can indeed be the case. How this scenario plays out depends upon which consensus becomes dominant, with the tacit hope that stability will again characterize society.

But the drive for stability can itself be an intrusive force for change, a force that tends to increase as common perceptions of instability increase. So drives for stability—the opinions for such directions—themselves only gain influence when they are held in a consensus. There is only one drive for stability that outlasts all of society's cycles, and that is religion. This persistence of religion is due to its perceived "unchangebleness". It always harkens to its roots, the ideal of stable times either lived by or described by the founder(s). This is a very powerful draw in times of chaos and instability, for religion calls to the very basic concepts of existence harbored by the spirit. And therein lies the source of religion's own plague of intrusive change, the spirit and its expression of individualism. For religion's "stability" is not tangible or palpable. One must deny reality for the most part and become dedicated as a "whole being" immersed in the faith that religion's stability is truth. Being then of spirit, religion's truth is subject to individual interpretation. As with other systems, if its precepts are generally accepted by popular consensus, that religion will be ascendant in society. If not, it will begin either to fractionate into competing interpretations or begin to be "diluted"—portions seen to have become irrelevant will be ignored.

So no system is truly stable. All are subject to the workings of what is called "Chaos Theory". What this means is that the behavior of a system is sensitively dependent upon its initial conditions, ie; its "track" as described above. Whenever an anomaly intrudes—that is, a change or new concept appears—a series of dislocations of conception spread across society, not unlike ripples radiating from a pebble's impact upon a pond's surface. Or, simply, a characteristic of an complex system is that an apparent status quo is upset by the introduction of an irregularity that results in turbulence. Inotherwords, the desired, or idealized, steady state of activity of a society (its "track") is brought to confusion by the introduction of change, or different conceptualizations.

The consequent turbulence—putting opinions to task and reorienting the consensi—is not entirely random or unpredictable. A people evolves with their society/civilization and so are inured to its environmentally shaped way of addressing the world and solving problems. Only when the introduction of an irregularity is accompanied by the infusion of a large number of foreigners who are inured to a different way of addressing the world and solving problems does the probability of randomness and unpredictability increase. Without this, however, below the turbulence an irregularity introduces, there are hidden regularities within the complex variety of a system's behavior. This is, of course, the track, that tacit guide that maintains a society's orientation short of complete collapse into chaos. If that happens, reliance on the soul comes to the fore, as humanity must exist at its most basic level to survive.

With the track related to its society's relationship to the world outside of it—that world that influenced its religion and formed its very social structure—it becomes very difficult to change. For changing the track would require an upheaval of society's most basic underpinnings: It means that a new environmental relationship with the surrounding world must be shaped. It means that God must assume a new aspect in order for the new environmental relationship to be made acceptable. Inotherwords, a new syncretism must develop so that the new track direction—or even a new track—can be successful. Only if this occurs can a society withstand great change.

Thus can we see the importance opinion plays in the competence, or survivability, or a civilization. It is not the day-to-day opinions that circulate throughout the population for these tend to be faddish, thriving on innuendo, gossip and attempts at being swayed. Not to be totally discounted, however, for these faddish opinions do indicate various individual's reflections on their relationship with their society's track. Rather is the "deeper" opinions, those that reflect orientation to the track and try to maintain society's "character". A society's (and so its civilization's) character is not unlike a system of fractals. That is; similar to Spencer's epicycles of small cycles make up larger cycles which make up larger cycles...etc: The whole is like its parts which are like their parts, etc. Each is similar and shares the same traits shaped by the track but influenced by regional (family, community,....) consensus. When the consensus is lost within several consensi that are themselves being enervated by opinions of increasing divergency, a society has lost direction. In periods wherein great change is challenging the track, a great cacophony of opinions only makes matters worse. Yet without this play of opinions, without a society-wide exposition of ideas, a determination of how the track should be reformed along with a new syncretism for society cannot be found. This period, or era, of conflicting opinions is what we have historically defined as a "Dark Age". It is a period of competing ideas, a struggle not unlike Darwin's "Survival of the Fittest". And the fittest would be that hoped for society with new character and new customs—a society that is once again stable. But opinion, whether it be political, economic, societal or personal, is usually an attempt to simplify complexity. Simplicity is seen as stability, which is construed as able to be translated into society itself. Post hunter-gatherer societies, however, have not been simple, having been themselves subject to the vicissitudes that change foists upon them. Thus the undercurrent of simplicity that drives a complex milieu of opinions is in itself a destabilizing factor. As many individuals seek simplicity via their various opinions, the development of a consensus is slowed. For a consensus necessitates the acceptance of complexity, allowing a greater number of individuals to accept it.

CHAPTER 5

Society and Social Darwinism

In very recent times, establishing a fairly solid position upon which to base an opinion by which the world is simplified has become somewhat difficult. Science and technology have quickly outpaced the rate at which humanity accepts and adapts to change. Yet the intrusion of change upon a society raises new ideas and so engenders new and different opinions. Such ideas and opinions aren't limited to an individual's relationship to society, but concern the world around him. And it is the world around us that has challenged us the most, presented change—almost demanding change: Opinions have been both a reflection of and effected by art, literature and music. These, but especially in these recent times, science and technology, have upset the very track that has served as opinion "director". Opinions, however, as the life blood of society, are the means by which the driving force of social evolution is realized. This driving force is competition—the engine of human advancement and development.

The manifestation of competition has been the deciding factor in societal survivability. Not only is the competition of ideas within a society necessary to define the consensus that will direct that society, but also the competition among the consensi of several societies. For a society can develop along a track, and express itself through its consensus, but its competitive worth, its survivability, is only decided when measured against other societies, other consensi. A most striking demonstration of this would be the domination of Europe over world history since about 1500.

The roots of this domination lie within that long period of gradual spreading conquest of Europe by the Indo-European peoples: From the Battle Axe Culture of Anatolia and the "Dorian Descent" of the Greek peninsula through the development of the Germanic and Celtic peoples that spread the Iron Age throughout the region, the nascent civilization and tribal rivalries of the region were overpowered by more forceful peoples. The female "Earth-Life" religions of the subcontinent were overrun by the more warlike male oriented (Earth-Domination) religion of these peoples. This domination was not complete, however, for the new was changed by the older religions which were adjusted to blend with the new. Thus the pantheism of Greece and Italy, though being male god dominated, had female gods that could wield some measure of power. Their religions were more benign, called to war as the need arose. Existence required a heartier vehicle in the more northern areas where life was more precarious. The pantheisms were thus more confrontational, more warlike—more competitive. It was this competitiveness that produced a European "mind set" that was not extinguished even after the Roman Church came to dominate the region. It set the stage for a Europe that was also a product of environment, ability of small societies to be fairly independent and an intense competition of ideas. This political diversity was largely due to geography. There were no enormous plains as in Asia, nor broad and fertile river zones as along the Ganges, Nile, Tigris, Euphrates, Yellow and Yangtze providing food for masses of toiling and easily conquerable peasants. Europe's landscape was more fractured with mountain ranges and forests separating populations; she was a haven of small areas delimited by rivers, mountains and/or the sea that were fairly easy to administer and keep fairly secure. Very similar to Mycenaean times that gave rise to Classical Greece; Europe in microcosm.

In addition, climate varies considerably from North to South and from East to West: All combined to make the establishment of unified control difficult—long term rule by a single entity was impossible. This variation encouraged growth and the continued existence of decentralized power, rule carried out by local kingdoms, marcher lordships, highland clans and lowland town confederations. Europe's political landscape looked like a fluctuating patchwork quilt. There was intense competition among these states and regions. Expansion of trade overland and especially by sea primarily of bulk goods and raw materials (as opposed to trade in luxury goods over Asian trade routes) led to entrepreneurships and trade organizations. Great commercial entrepreneurships arose, from the Hanseatic League to the singular endeavors of Genoa and Venice. Trade and industry flourished under the auspices of secularism that gave free reign to competitiveness. Unlike Asia where such things were strictly controlled by clerical rules of morality and life that tended to attenuate any no-holds barred competition.

The result of free trade and competition was the beginning characteristics of today's modern economy. Bills of exchange, a credit system and international banking were developed. Merchantile credit and bills of insurance pointed toward predictability of economic systems, enjoyed by merchants nowhere else in the world. This nascent world economy was fueled in large part by trade by sea, much of which was carried out between the Mediterranean and North Sea and beyond. Storms and need for ever larger cargo capacities pushed the development of sturdier, longer-ranging ships.

Perhaps the greatest impetus to European superiority was through this decentralized and unsupervised growth of commerce, merchants, ports and markets. These economic developments were never fully suppressed. By 1500 most of the regimes of Europe had entered into a symbiotic relationship with the market economy, providing domestic order and a non-arbitrary legal system—and receiving taxes and a share in the growth of trade. With unrestrained trade, increased carrying capacity of ships and the growing amount of bulk goods moving about the continent, some means of increasing the efficiency of manufacture was needed. Science, technology and mathematics—court curiosities and hobbies of the nobility elsewhere—become tools that enabled this efficiency to be achieved: The Industrial Revolution was the result.

The environmental conditions (weather, water, flora, fauna, geography and geology) that fueled this dynamic competitiveness both mirrored and were mirrored by mankind's evolutionary change from the physical to the social. In Europe, this transition was depicted in an acculturation that was becoming more human-oriented rather than to nature. Through science and technology, mankind could almost predict—or more closely with the growth of statistical sophistication—seasonal and other physical conditions around him. Nature was becoming familiar—"handleable"—allowing human's environmental orientation to become more mental than physical. This was evident not only to his cultural development (art, literature, music, etc.) but also to his emerging societal forms; his governments, economies and as we have seen, his religion. Despite the forms taken by emerging cultures, they all, as we have seen, develop a "set" because each societal form is the most efficient relationship with its environment possible at that time. There are then efforts to maintain this set because the benefits that were realized in the beginning want to be continued. So with the intrusion of change, the set is challenged and Darwinian forces are set in motion.

Since mankind's evolutionary focus has changed from the physical to the social, his Darwinian forces have changed to Social Darwinism. This is a far more complex situation than the standard biological evolutionary process we are used to. The birth, growth and ongoing existence of society/civilization involves a very complex interrelationship of science and technology, culture and economics, religion and political philosophy that would only change at a rate commensurate with a normal ageing process. Inotherwords, just like our bodies, the ageing process is a series of adjustments as various parts become used to different wear patterns, gravitational forces and habitual movements. Changes are slowly introduced, and as they are, the rest of the body easily accepts them. More abrupt changes, however, call into play the body's competence. Some diseases, for example, can be easily fought off while others may be quite traumatic, placing the body in such stress that its natural defenses cannot withstand the onslaught. The result may be permanent debility or even death.

A society is much the same, though its commitment to its "set" will determine how disruptive an introduced change will be. The Hanseatic League, for example, had a good thing going. So it controlled commerce and managed to influence much government economic policy so that its benefits continued. But the world was changing; the Hanse's policies—while beneficial to itself—were becoming more suppressive of the economic freedom of those countries and communes that at first reaped much benefit from it. Eventually governments began passing laws regulating the Hanse's practices, and in other instances used military force to suppress it.

It is much the same when a society's/civilization's consensus is challenged at a rate greater than it can absorb and adjust. Reactions, as we have seen, set it: The overall consensus breaks down as individual opinions—directed by genetic structure and reaction to personal environments—diverge, embroiled in a grand melee attempting to coalesce into a new consensus. Plato believed this process follows a pattern: Societies move from Monarchy to Democracy to Dictatorship ("every democracy votes itself into dictatorship") and finally back to Monarchy. With a stretch of imagination, one could say history bears this out. While history may show that there have been trends in this direction, and the consensi of a fractured consensus may display such trends, mankind's evolution has been such that it is impossible to "go back" to what was. From the very days when humans became toolmakers, the collection of information and empirical data has been growing at an ever accelerating rate. Beliefs and practices based on erroneous or incomplete information became impossible to reintroduce with the discovery of the facts concerning them.

So a societies age, as their knowledge about the world in which they exist accumulates, the attitude of their competence changes. It is presumed that greater knowledge increases choices and courses of adaptability. Such adaptiveness is evident when a society is not beset by intrusive change. The slow change in the meanings of words, for example, reflect change in individual's conceptualization of their society. Conceptualization that is interrelated with knowledge gain, life style changes, and the relationship of the individual to his society as it changes through the normal ageing process. Thus can be seen why laws must be changed, for what was appropriate at one time becomes either passe or reprehensible later. With more intrusive change, the "set" is challenged, and laws may be changed to reflect the consensus' resistance. Such is fare for the rise and fall of governments, as we saw above. For society's ultimately reflect the attitudes (consensus) of their citizenry, and if those attitudes resist instead of trying to adapt to change, those society's competency may be called into question.

For example, with the breakdown of society due to a divergency of opinions from intrusive change, the tacit cooperation of community also breaks down. The unwritten codes of morality, conduct and consideration begin to be tested. Spirit begins to move more personalities into areas heretofore relegated to the lesser populated regions of society's bell curves (attribute "tracks"—in the next chapter): Crime and other unsatisfactory behavior begins an increase beyond their normal percentages. The difficulty in this is that being Spirit driven—ie; formed from the environment of social milieu that is changing by the reaction from the intrusive change—the perpetrators do not consider themselves an aberration. No one performs an act that does not seem justifiable to him. That act can be murder, rape, child molestation, giving to charity, volunteer work, running for public office, terrorism, espousing a certain religion or philosophical view, etc, etc; no matter, the performance of that act will be justified by the performer. That it may be a reprehensible act to the majority does not discount the perpetrator's justification.

Changes in morality, or changes of location of the line separating acceptable from unacceptable acts, are more complicated. Moral conventions and law are usually tied in with social law and religion. While changes in moral convention accompany the evolving changes in word meanings along with slowly changing applications of the law, religious change is far more difficult. There are two reasons for this; one is that religion holds Spirit's defining of our reason for being. Since Spirit doesn't have the comfort of nature to fall back upon, its determination of God and the reason for being stand alone. Any attempt to change this leaves it without any other frame of reference to use in establishing different or new ones.

A second difficulty religion has is that it is codified in Holy Books. Unlike the law that can be changed in concert with evolving word meanings, to change word meanings in a holy book is to alter the original concept of the religion. So we can see why religion quickly (in historical terms) loses its relevance after its founding days. With ageing societies—their accumulation of knowledge, changing word meanings and evolving societal relationships—religion soon becomes an increasingly conservative brake on societal evolution. Yet even this stalwart resistance to change has not always withstood the social pressures when it has been part of an intrusive change. Whether it be Buddhism, Judaism, Christianity, Islam, Hinduism or any other, their movement into society's that evolved with completely different characteristics of the relationship of nature/religion/society were themselves altered in character. These other (more "primitive") societies or regions reinterpreted the intrusive religion so as to strike a balance that didn't threaten their evolved Spirit concept of reason for being. Sort of a compromise religion/moral standard was the result; the relationship to God, ritual practices, interpretation of holy writ and acceptable moral acts—all somewhat different than the original religion—were the result. The name, however, remained, so that even a compromised religion could still be claimed to be part of the original.

An assertion can be made that religion and moral law are self-destructive. That their inability to accept or adapt to change as rapidly as can the societies of which they are part, decreases their society's competitiveness. This only because they are so slow to change in concert with evolving law and society. Note that public opinion and the evolving consensus relating to law and morality are not necessarily the same. Public opinion can be faddish which, as we have seen, can tend to head a consensus or one of the consensi off in dangerous directions. When an intrusive change challenges a society, in general, divergencies of opinion are created and the breakup of the consensus begins. This is even more troubling for religion and morality, for they deal with a "higher" ethics and consider every push to expand or alter what is "normal" or "proper" a breakdown of society. Indeed, a challenged consensus does not necessarily mean that society is breaking down, just that it must come to terms with new circumstances. A breakdown is what the Dark Age—or Age of Adjustment—may seem like, but, as we have seen, it is merely thrashing about in search of a new consensus.

How behavior changes, or acts that "cross the line", are approached by society can themselves create changes of conditions that may be unacceptable to many, thereby constituting an intrusive change. While repression by penalty and punishment may deter many from performing these acts, the pressures to perform these acts are nonetheless still there. What must be accomplished is an alteration of Spirit so that one cannot justify performing these acts. Thus true reduction of unacceptable acts can only come through societal reform. Psychology, the science of the future, will, when its validity is acknowledged by almost all (human nature precludes 100% acceptability!), will enable various behaviors to be modified thereby reducing incidences of aberrant behavior. Eventually modification won't be the goal, for the general tenor of relationships within society expressed by psychology will become normal. This will then enable each individual's relationship with his society to approach some sort of an ideal.

This relationship between the citizenry and their society is called a "Social Contract". It does not matter what form any society takes—it can range from repressive to chaotically liberal—its citizens adjust, becoming inured to its idiosyncrasies. Becoming part of their society's "set", their acceptance constitutes a sort of contract. That is, they presume conditions will not change too radically as they have adjusted their lives and projected their future conditions based on present conditions—the "set". But within the normal range of evolution, when gradual change takes place, the many relationships among individuals and those between individuals and the aggregate whole—their society also change. Thus the contract is fluid like the rest of mankind's societies; nothing is ever really "set" as in stasis because of the accumulation of knowledge—part of mankind's progression toward separation from nature, which is the cellular aim of achieving security. There is also the natural ageing process; since all slowly readjust through a ageing process; the social contract is not immune. This natural changing through normal ageing is strained by intrusive change, so not only is society beset by challenges, but the very relationships among individuals are challenged. This results in a slow evolution in defining the social contract itself: What **are** the relationships individuals have with each other and their government/society. Indeed, what is going to be the new (or re-) definition of our society?

There have been two great "revolutions" or periods of phenomenal intrusive change during mankind's tenure. The first, of course, was agricultural in which whole aspects of societies were forced to undergo alteration—indeed many new aspects that hadn't existed during hunter-gatherer days had to be defined. The second revolution is one that isn't yet over, but that is having a far greater and thoroughgoing impact on mankind's societies than had the first. Industrialization, accompanied by a rapid growth of information dissemination (from moveable type to computerization) and scientific method (based upon mathematical sophistication) have brought us to a point where the economics of competition is increasingly defining our societies' parameters. Changing from agricultural to industrial economies (where agriculture has become "industrialized") has forced development of new rules defining the position of those who must provide labor for the "system" within their society. Early on, several economic philosophers, Marx, Smith, Gournay, Quesnay, Mirabeau, Turgot, Dupont de Nemours among others, sought to define either this new relationship or (of which the new relationship is apart) the ideal workings of this nascent economic system. The twentieth century has seen the penultimate act in the viability—fitness—of economic systems. Communism and Capitalism battled throughout almost the whole century, with capitalism eventually outperforming communism. Now the conflict will be between United States' styled capitalism and European styled capitalism. This will be one of the greatest sources of social uncomfortableness ever seen, because redefining an economic system both impacts and is impacted by the many relationships that make up the Social Contract. Each is intruding on the other; there is much dialogue, praise and criticism. At heart it is the ultimate relationship between citizen and society that is to be decided: Each's "set" is being challenged by the other. The American system is thought not to "do enough" for its people ("you don't get much for your taxes"); social programs are lean and sparse, there is under and unemployment, poverty and low educational achievement. The European system is more far reaching than this, thought by many Americans to be too "socialistic" in its attempts to alleviate these problems—to actually take Roussou's "Social Contract" to heart. Yet each is beset by problems that have come from centuries of intrusive change, including that of industrialization. Two of these, though related, are loss of humanity and crime.

Crime, or more widely, violence, have been a part of mankind as far back as we can ascertain. For as much as we are against violence and try to stamp it out, it does play a role. While it was addressed by ancients from China to Rome—satirized by Suetonius in fact—only recently has it become an alarming situation due to the omniscience of modern communication. Yet this has been part of the normal milieu of human society, and on of the measures of its ability to survive.

There has always been pedophilia, children raped, infanticide, kidnapping, parental brutality and molestation, and mutilation of young females (perhaps originally a crude attempt at birth control?). Modern psychology has developed a case for the reactions visited upon the individuals from these horrors. Yet these are really tests as to the viability of society. In the general character of society—its "community spirit" if you will how people who have undergone these tribulations are accepted into society is a measure of that society's fitness to survive. This "spiritual support" that enables the victims to live and work out their traumas measures the health of a society. Its somewhat similar to comparing a society's health—strength of competence, or fitness to survive—with the relationship between our bodies and disease. Unlike the body, however, how society handles violence is not a natural function of a complex cellular organization fighting an intruder, or disease. A society's response to violence is determined by its consensus that is being shaped by the aggregate of many opinions. When a society allows itself to become bogged down by violence, descending into its lower levels, its fitness to survive is challenged. For this is, as Rousseau states, a "return to nature" and a retrograde movement in relation to the steady direction of mankind's evolution. It is as though a society in this state sows the seeds of its own destruction. For these barbarities serve to attenuate population growth, especially in modern times for our own species—one that has developed means to eliminate its natural limitations—disease, infant mortality and female death during childbirth.

The trauma of child molestation, rape, parental brutality, etc, poisons ability to form healthy relationships that produce individuals suitable enough to carry on civilization. For this behavior visits upon generations born into it a citizenry of declining associative conceptualization of their civilization. This is the final challenge to the consensus: How will society react? How will it restructure itself to restore associativeness within the consensus? Here is the measure of mankind's worth—man's evolution having evolved from physical to social—that social quality is tested. Especially present conditions that are exacerbated by "progress" wrought by the industrial/technological revolution: As the modern state has progressed to reduce the despair, sadness and tragedies that can occur in people's lives, the rise of violence tends to assure their remaining.

The industrial/technological states have raised to higher degrees than ever seen before the necessity for the elimination of emotion. The very nature of these—industrialization and technology—based as they are on mathematics and inductive processes—dictates order and methodical deliberation. Their aim is predictability and future results through today's planning. If human emotions are allowed a part in this scheme, a measure of unpredictability is added. And such unpredictability can have varying results—from an inconsequential annoyance to popular motivation that can cripple an economic structure.

For centuries philosophers have decried the dehumanization that characterizes advanced civilizations. It is no different today. The methodical proceduralism of operating an industrial/ technological society is not unlike operating a slave-based system. In fact, all that has happened is the substitution of machines for slaves. But this dehumanization is a reaction to the future of civilization. Humanity's development of the modern civilization has far outpaced its need to evolve with it. Just as civilization arose within a symbiosis among religion, environment, agricultural requirements and governmental organization, the evolution of our future society must also evolve in the same way. But the pace of industrial and technological development is pushing mankind toward his future faster than most can readily accept. Within this methodical society, emotion becomes an intrusive change. Without any orientation toward emotional states— that is, without latitudinal allowances for human emotional response—individuals turn to violence, for only that emotional expression elicits a societal response. And so, as discussed above, how society responds to this condition—that is, what is the consensual response—will determine the face of Social Darwinism: Will it become communitive, bringing understanding and group participation to reduce violence to an allowable statistical norm? Or will it become repressive, raising anew the forces that have driven history to record the rise and fall of nations?

Just as mankind's evolution is changing from the physical to the social—where society changes and evolves instead of the physical body—so too are the mechanisms of that society. The emotion of hunter-gatherer tribalism is being transformed into a new Panessence of an one-world community. It will become apparent that this new community will have an organization quite unlike to what we are accustomed. The Panessence will be a primary factor, for emotionalism, violence and other natural pressures will not exist.

CHAPTER 6

The Ending Dark Age

The mechanisms of society only operate to the benefit of its population when they are an expression of the consensus. But genetics and an individual's environment—be it family, community or the consensus itself—can move Spirits to veer in different directions. This is not to suggest that things move along smoothly until a disruption scatters individualistic thinking. Human society is a kaleidoscope of shifting, changing, merging, separating and compromising opinions about any and every factor that makes it up. In this way it is indeed quite a fragile mechanism, requiring responsibility and sacrifice to make it work. It is easier to revert—as Locke and Rousseau said, "to Nature", but most of mankind eschew the brutality this envisions. Perhaps the best way to demonstrate the kaleidoscopic nature of society is to consider bell curves. Let us take **one** attribute of the population of a society, say, for example, the state of being comfortable, and apply it to a bell curve. The curve is plotted on a graph with its vertical axis as population from 0 to 50%, and the horizontal measuring the state of the attribute for each person. The total population is the area under the curve. For our example the fewest numbers will be among those who'll say either just having enough to fill their belly is comfort or to be so fabulously wealthy that their every need is satisfied. But the great majority will lie in between these two extremes, with the greatest number having minimal differences in their conceptions of comfort. The bell curve reflects this in its shape; the greatest percentage of population with more or less similar conceptions occupy the center. Now consider that society is made up of a great number of bell curves. Any attribute that can be thought of upon which people would have an opinion—from the meaning of words to morality, from religious convictions to politics, from the definition of culture to economics, etc, etc—will have a bell curve distribution for that population. And not every person will be found on the same place on all of these bell curves. When times are chaotic or the people are in the throes of a "dark age", when intrusive change disrupts a society's orderliness, individual positions on a wide number of subjects vary considerably. This creates bell curves with less amplitude —a flatter shape that describes wide ranging opinions and the lack of consensus—for the individuals within that population are found scattered all over them. When increasing numbers of people begin to share similarities of opinions on various subjects, they begin to show up at more or less the same positions on pertinent bell curves. The curves then begin to increase in amplitude, assuming more of their characteristic bell shape. This means that a consensus begins to emerge. This is what occurred as history recorded the rise of great religions, the rise of great cultural movements, and even of governments themselves, each a coordination of those bell curve attributes that created a consensus that allowed them to form.

It is interesting to note that bell curve amplitude and coordination is cyclic in nature. Plato wrote about the evolution of governments, and while history has not exactly born this out, he was in a way describing societal cyclicality. A cycle occurs when a certain percentage of a population share similar attribute positions on pertinent bell curves. If the number of people sharing this bell curve position increase, the curve's amplitude increases so that a shared opinion becomes a movement, then one of the consensi, then a consensus. Meanwhile, the other attributes with low amplitudes are tumbling about, reacting off one another, as the search for another one of the consensi struggle on. One's position on any particular bell curve, however, is not etched in stone. Since humans are members of the only surviving types—Homo sapiens sapiens, or anatomically modern humans—they are all more or less the same. Part of their survival technique—since human evolution has changed from physical to social—is to revise their opinions. By applying intellectual forces on their bell-curve positions, humans are able to adapt and modify, even to accept other positions. Thus bell-curve positions are flexible, and can change as individual's react in their own particular way to social conditions around them. What these social conditions are, indeed what the characteristics of a society are in general, and what range of differences are found throughout a population, are largely determined by the manner in which society's attributes are (or are not) transmitted from generation to generation.

The so-called "higher" animals must have a training period for their young in order to learn those activities too complex to be handled by instinct alone. Among the most highly developed are humans, for their society—after having become separated from nature—relies far less on instinct than it does on learned behavior. Thus human society is a function of individual's thought processes: A consensus can only emerge from a majority of similar thought processes that will raise the amplitude of the bell curves. Since this is passed on from generation to generation, the manner—physical, psychological and cultural—in which the young are trained sets the course for either establishing or maintaining the nature of the consensus. How individuals or a population behaves in the various circumstances in which they find themselves is determined by how society's tenets are maintained through the generations. There are no true "standards" of behavior, however, or reactions to circumstances, but social psychology has outlined general parameters of how humans in general react to certain conditions. With humans being fairly similar, their reactions to the ebb and flow of historical phenomena are also fairly similar. This is reflected in their movements among bell-curves, producing the cyclicality of trends and similarities of consensi. The old adage "History repeats itself" reflects this. Or in Santayana's maxim implying the predictability of these historical cycles, "Those ignorant of history are doomed to repeat it". But, as we have seen, there is never an exact repetition since knowledge and experience is cumulative. The expression of community/society/ civilization as recorded by history has been a record of consistent intrusion by change that has never allowed stasis. Similarities natural to human individuals and their thought processes have persisted in pressures for agreement that have been manifested in the more or less cyclicality of the historical record. Now, in the ending period of our Dark Age, the cycles are becoming fully uncoordinated. The intrusion of change, widely known by the omniscience of information delivery and retrieval, has placed under world-wide scrutiny practically the whole range of society's parameters.

For the sake of brevity, the only parameters to be considered here will be economics, relationship with the environment, social states, education and religion. Since society developed as a product of their interrelationship, the best way to estimate their prognosis is to consider them in the overall. So by following the evolutionary thread of history we are able to understand our long Dark Age. This can be done by following the historical record and tracing conditions that led to the decline of today's "world" governments: Those nation states that have carried humanity from the Renaissance to the present as though they were "worlds unto themselves" are now becoming victims of intrusive change and are themselves also resisting those forces. Not unlike individuals, their own self-interests are being threatened, and so they fear the uncertainty of any "new" order. But this has been a long ongoing process and its complexities can be somewhat confusing. For government—or the organization of society as acceded to by the consensus—is, as has been discussed, part of the symbiosis of religion, environment and economic policy that characterizes a society/civilization. Perhaps nowhere else in history has the disruption of change and resistance to it been so constant as in government's story. It is not a smooth evolutionary story, however, for it is replete with advances, retrograde movements and confusion. Evidenced by, as has been discussed, the kaleidoscopic expression of reaction to events expressed by the many bell curves of human attributes. Yet, generally, intrusive change has been very much a part of governmental development that can be described as having followed seven general phases.

First would be named **Clerical**, not much government but an intimate association with its environment. This would be early Neolithic, hunter-gatherer type societies where survival hinges on a religious adherence to the ways of the natural world. The hunter-gatherer society is egalitarian, so government is simple and clerics few, consisting of simple personages called today shamans, or medicine men, etc. Their function is to assure the smoothest possible interrelationship between the people and their environment, an ecological coexistence they share intimately through their animistic religion. In this society, the people are generalists, everyone is able to perform all of the tasks necessary to make the community work. What little specialization there is occurs in those areas dictated by sex (the classic "woman home cooking/birthing—men out hunting/defending") and of course the shamans. Intrusive change is minimal, coming mainly from intertribal contacts. About the only great stresses placed upon this society are difficulties that would arise from irregularities in the yearly seasonal progression. Being generalists and highly mobile allows rapid adaptation to such occurrences, and only if environmental change is severe would traumatic stresses be experienced. Their economy is also environmentally related; location dictates availability of raw materials and so trade by barter is the system used. Generally, however, this is minimal, for hunter-gatherer societies are structured for the best ecological fit with their environment. Education too reflects this, as the young are taught the ways of society mainly by experience—sort of an apprenticeship method.

Mankind's longest time spent during his existence was as hunter-gatherers. While other mammals demonstrate very similar societies (chimpanzees, baboons, wolves, etc), the added character for humans was the separation from nature. Separation meant the beginning of a declining reliance on individuals connected by soul, though hunter-gatherers retain far more than more advanced societies. The shortfall was made up of language, very simple with limited vocabulary, that enabled spirits to be connected and express those things known instinctively by the soul. But more importantly, the historical trace leading to the present, was begun at this time. This long period of pre-history saw the emergence of toolmaking, perhaps the greatest technological step taken. It forever set mankind's course on a pattern of development that required further development to make up for an increasing distance from a natural orientation.

This increasing distance, or increasing lack of natural orientation, added a new factor to his religious ideas that came to hold an increasing influence over his cultural and economic development. For now mankind was required to explain his existence and how he and the world about him came about. For by this time—well into the hunter-gatherer stage—mankind had so long been separate from nature, having lost association with the continuity (within evolution) of existence within its context that a plausible explanation became necessary. So it was during the first phase—no doubt with roots that reached long before—that stories of Creation materialized. This was a Spirit led quest, for Soul had no reason for devising such a scheme, being wholly oriented to nature. But spirit was without a locus and had to manufacture one, so a system that explained how mankind came about, indeed how the world in which he lived came about, was devised. For reasons mentioned above—environmental, geographical, climatological, etc.—these stories varied from region to region. But their essence was similar; a species that lost its orientation to nature had to devise the how and why of its existence.

Soon to arise after determining the creation was to determine the true nature of mankind. This was a problem that was to plague humanity through all of history, for new knowledge, new outlooks fostered by intrusive change and the natural evolutionary changes in civilization continued to alter the factors upon which a definition of mankind's being were based. So began the endless confusion of misunderstanding the true nature of man—not so much as a highly developed organization of cells but—as a being of nature whose reality lies within the scope of natural law and its processes. This was replaced by trying to define the soul with volition and the manner in which it relates to the creation and subsequent society and its laws. Death was no longer accepted as a function of living—"immortality" is gained through the continuation of the species—but as the end of one "stage" from which the "soul" went to the next. These stories of creation and the nature of mankind formed a disruptive undercurrent of self-inflicted intrusive change that both affected and were affected by human technological advancement.

Further development saw a tremendous technological maturity that was surprisingly sophisticated for societies without writing or the organizational trends we associate with advanced civilization. Tools of stone, bone, wood and antler were produced; there was stone carving, cave wall painting; needles, pins, jewelry, fish traps, fairly sophisticated buildings and the beginnings of megalithic construction. So the merge into mankind's second phase was really just an evolution of sophistication development (coupled of course with the environmental needs that spurred the onset of agriculture). This phase is called **Clerical/ Secular**, and corresponds to the period from the Neolithic to the Bronze Age. Secular power makes its appearance as the demands of farming, harvesting, storage, irrigation, trade and defense require a more complex society, one that requires greater organization for these non-religious functions. As with any entity with a certain organization, intrusive change becomes a concern as the status quo, or "set", of society during this stage is quite well developed. Already, the adaptability of hunter-gatherer has been lost, traded for organizational steadiness and evident need to restructure the environment to fit. All post hunter-gatherer political/economic systems developed dependent upon some measure of environmental exploitation. In this clerical/secular phase, there are some efforts of control (mainly irrigation works) but there remains much acceptance of the whims of nature. A measure of control was desired, however, over nature's unpredictability and this was what religion attempted to do. The passivity of animistic spiritualism was transferred into a more mankind-serving belief: Animism coalesced into a mother-goddess dominated pantheon toward which appeals could be made for desired ends (good harvest, good weather, plenty of fish and fauna, victory over enemies, etc.) or a beneficial life could be had by adhering to the pantheon's rules. It can be easily seen how government during this phase is a function of religion. The animistic spirits of before could no longer be related to the governmental functions that an organized society required. Yet government and the results of its workings (defense, harvest, water supply, popular welfare, etc.) was just as dependent on working with the pantheon as was everyone else.

The social status of the clerical/secular phase is characterized by the rise of clerical and royal power. As society's complexity increased during this phase, greater organization of non-religious functions was required. Specialization was becoming common and so too a bureaucracy. Besides providing a steady administrative hand that orchestrated the interrelationships of specialties, the bureaucracy also attenuated any upsetting policy changes that could occur if a change of ruler brought a mercurial temper to the throne. Bureaucracy, though, was a clerical function during this phase, since the pantheon had to be properly propitiated—demonstrated through proper government actions—to assure the harvest, popular welfare, etc.

Still another great change from hunter-gatherer society was the sophistication of economics. With the decrease of hunting as a main source of food and the rise of agriculture concomitant with specialization, there was a tremendous growth of both trade and manufacturing. While labor was mostly by serfs or slaves, there arose a new class of people, the entrepreneurs, who developed a wealth base and therefore some political power through their trade and manufacturing. Known today as the Bourgeoisie, they were independent investors who usually under the auspices of the religious establishment provided a beneficial service or commodity. Their role and numbers were very small during this phase, however, for the religious establishment controlled the bureaucracy and thereby controlled most of society's economy.

Since labor was mostly unskilled, educational needs were by apprenticeship: Whether it was trade acumen, pottery or tool making, jewelry and cloth making, or even secretarial and positions in the bureaucracy, were easily handled through apprenticeship. Everything was "low tech" and labor intensive, so this was a suitable way of passing on skills. Toward the end of this period, writing began to appear, yet even here apprenticeship was utilized though under very strict control so that the meanings of words did not change. The epitome one could achieve from an education during this phase would be a position within the clerical hierarchy, for this meant a position of power and influence.

Being but the first step beyond hunter-gatherer, the clerical/ secular phase was still quite beholden to its environment. Survival, however, required some attempts to manipulate these conditions, the most notable being irrigation works and Earth oriented—mother goddess— tombs and temples. This manipulation was under the guidance of religious officials as they could "read signs"; that is, interpret conditions to best predict the future. Being able to do this placed them as a group in a powerful position in society. Another powerful group was the bourgeoisie: They were traders, entrepreneurs and some of the nobility whose wealth, like that of the clergy, provided them with a position of power. The Bronze Age was uniquely geared toward this rising group as bronze production was an expensive business. It was some of the nobility that benefitted the most as they owned or controlled those lands having copper and tin deposits. If these deposits weren't within a country's borders, ownership was obtained by warfare or trade agreements would secure adequate supplies. At this time, however, many rulers were forced to curtail or restrict the power of both the bourgeoisie and nobility/clergy. For they tended to exploit the poorer citizens and it was in the interests of civil harmony that such practices did not go too far. So rulers from Enmebaragisi, Naram Sin, Sargon the Great and others issued codes of law that tried to instill a measure of fairness in society. This, of course, created its own detrimental force of change as the bourgeoisie and clerical/nobility reacted against what they perceived as unfair controls upon them. All in all, however, the general state of society followed a fairly regular pattern. Mankind was just trying out his presumed independence from nature and did not vary much in these first tentative steps into the unknown. There was a reluctance to upset the status quo, and so bell curve differences were minimal. But as has been discussed, knowledge is cumulative, and as the scope of knowledge broadens beyond what an individual can easily understand, the impetus for bell curve divergence grows as focuses narrow. Slowly, pressures build for individualism (ie; bell curve position) to be more openly expressed.

Just this sort of thing characterized the next, or third, phase—called **Secular/Clerical**. Historically this period roughly covers the rise of iron (the "iron age") to the end of Rome/Han/ Gupta. There was a great increase in intrusive change to which reaction was less easily contained. One of these was the spread of iron technology; its cheapness disrupted the "elite" nobility and bourgeoisie that dominated the bronze economies by widening the ability of others to challenge their power: Iron was widely available, the ores more easily reduced and the product worked ("anyone" could be a blacksmith!). Mankind's approach to his environment also changed, as iron allowed larger armies to be equipped at less cost per man to expand and/or protect trade routes, mining and agricultural areas. There was an intensification of trade traffic as widely available iron hardware made better wagons and ships possible, and as cheaper iron tools enabled agriculture to be carried out by a greater number of people and spread over greater areas. The intrusive change this engendered was quite profound, as was the reaction to it. As agricultural and economic spheres spread, the stability of established government and society—including its religion—was needed to maintain the accustomed order. Governments became world governments, or empires, thereby setting in motion a trend of bell curve position dislocations that have never fully recovered to this day. As these great world governments expanded, there was contact with other societies, other religions, other environments that required adjustments of normalcy in order to survive them and of course other world governments. The pressures for change these contacts created were enormous. The farther afield a great government's control was extended, the more diffuse it became, blending somewhat with local standards that allowed outlying peoples to retain a semblance of independence. Among more progressive rulers, there dawned a primitive realization of world interrelatedness and they would retain defensive perimeters, trade routes and raw material supplies (ie; loyalties) through diplomacy. Most, however, chose the more direct approach of war. This spread of government organization with both a need for and increase of economic needs and reorganization, increased needs for environmental cooperation. Obtaining this was largely impossible as ability to control the environment due to lack of technology and knowledge was limited mainly to roads, irrigation works and wall building. So desire for greater control that was physically impossible rested on reliance on religion. This increasing reliance on religion to gain spiritual control of the environment brought it into being a useful arm of the government. This became a necessity as a society's efficiency was envisioned as having a unity of belief among—and demanded of—its people. Not only was this necessary in order to obtain environmental acquiescence but also for political presence: If a society displayed any division or divisiveness, this was considered a sign of weakness.

During this phase religion was also undergoing changes. While the phases were changing, there was an evolution of the female oriented mother-goddess religion into a more "equi-sex" pantheism wherein calling upon certain deities made carrying out warfare or destructive environmental acts justifiable. Inotherwords, some deities were domineering and warlike, while others were more cerebral, compromising and supportive of peaceful methods. As this phase was coming toward its end, however, growing societal pressures were making this religious status untenable. So a more "worldly view" religion was needed that corresponded with the great world state: The size of the "core" civilization that people could consider themselves part of was much larger than the areas of the last phase. This new core civilization, being now "world" wide, needed a religion to match. But since there was such diversity encountered in establishing this core civilization, religion had to be as powerful as the great states in order to impress its truth upon outlying regions. So a period began—overlapping into the next phase—that saw the birth of the warrior religions of Brahmanism, Judaism, Christianity and Mohammedanism. Here were religions of power heretofore unheard of. Theirs was the ability to meld this new self proclaimed power with world unifying and environment taming powers (or assumed powers) of the great governments. Their growth underwrote the spread of one-world governments that were to some extent efforts to prevent chaos from the very intrusive change they encountered.

With the spread of one-world religions and the attempted domination of one-world (at least as large as possible) governments, the resultant chaos touched every aspect of human civilization. These conditions forced a renewed examination of meaning and reality. While the growing one-world religions had updated the creationism of the previous phase yet not altering the soul's definition much, others began to examine reality a little differently. At the forefront of this examination were ideas emerging in the Hellenistic region that stretched from Italy to northern India. This was the beginning of the separation of religion and philosophy, beginning an occasionally acrimonious dispute that sometimes influenced and was influenced by the secular pursuits of civilization. The ensuing debate defining reality, perception of reality, soul and/or being and the importance or relevance of god lasted well into the fifth phase.

Although having never been separate, during this phase economics and civilization's social state became more closely intertwined. Agriculture was of course king, and while there were many yeomen farmers, the bulk of foodstuffs came from great landed estates or dukedoms maintained by slave labor. Manufacturing, however, was quite extensive, but is reached its limitations due to the limitations of technology and flesh power. Two things occurred here; economic existence demanded a great amount of finely divided specialization and clerical subservience to a great, complex (bureaucratic) secular government necessary to coordinate relationships among the specialties. Clerical organization, having become a useful arm of the government was thus itself a specialty, and so became somewhat subservient to the secular government as increasing trade, defense and other international dealings demanded a more powerful, efficient government.

Society began to acquire a "set", however, for the greater the organization evolved to maintain order among the specialties, the more difficult it became to introduce change. And both the bourgeoisie and nobility who realized a high standard of living form the great incomes the earned were wary of any change that may jeopardize this condition. For several generations it seemed like things would go on without change; a sort of status quo was reached. Leisure time became available to the upper classes so they either dabbled in or underwrote the arts, games and various cultural pursuits. They monopolized education which, besides the still prevalent apprenticeships for many avocations, now saw actual schools. These taught basics—mainly religion (with some philosophy) and writing—to scions of the upper classes in order to perpetuate their cultural pursuits.

As the drive to establish vast "world" governments strove to include all the several finite known worlds, internal evolutionary developments as well as border contacts created a crisis of spirit far more intense than in the previous phases. The great wealth these civilizations accumulated was held in large part among not only the nobility but also both the clerical establishment and the entrepreneurial bourgeoisie. Maintaining their influential position and economic well being meant a hardening insistence on maintaining the status quo. This was in conflict with an accelerating input of intrusive change that bombarded these wide-ranging societies straining beyond normal variance the coordination of bell curves necessary for civilization's continuance. Most of this bell curve discordance took place among the nobility and bourgeoisie. Especially the latter who, having gained a semblance of independence by their wealth, were convinced they didn't really need any government to secure their wellbeing—ignoring conditions that evolved from the very governmental organization they eschew of which they were shrewd enough to take advantage. The bell curve disruption that increased during this phase was not as freewheeling as it seems: Mankind's collective experience was not yet wide enough to engender any great shifts in concept. There was moral and family breakdown (ie; Petronius' **Satyricon**) and in general the spreading of those traits outlined by Gibbon that characterize a declining civilization. Yet the core intrinsicality of civilization—reliance and belief in religion and the monarchy, a tacit acceptance of the "caste" of one's place in society— were maintained. For the most part, the lower classes held to this core, of morality, of family, of religion and of monarchy—and the monarchs usually did their best in catering to this lower class solidarity, which enabled them to maintain some control over sometimes overzealous nobles, clergy and bourgeoisie. This was the state of affairs as the next phase began.

Moving into the next phase, the fourth, was rather sudden in relation to the general pace of historical evolution. Called the **Secular/Clerical Breakdown**, it was characterized either by or both massive invasions and the disintegration common to an absence of bell-curve accordance. It would correspond to the European Medieval (or "Dark Age"), Indian post-Gupta and Chinese era of Five Dynasties and 16 states. The great "world states" broke up as they were slammed by a double blast of intrusive change: Both societies and economies were disrupted by invasions and discordant bell-curves preventing formation of any consensus to withstand these forces. Intrusive change was rampant, far too much for the "world" governments to withstand. Their great civilization exuded wealth, that to outsiders, who saw in their fractious societies with leaders who have become effete from the power of wealth and not will, have become easy pickings. These changes broke up the social cohesiveness of the old governments. A new tribalism emerged as civilization balkanized, breaking up into small communities—towns, cities and larger areas ruled by minor barons or clerics. There was a retreat into moral, social and religious conservatism in order to "hang onto" what was left of the old civilization. Inotherwords, society closed down so as to keep out further change while searching for a new consensus. As this phase progressed, a minimization of the almost traumatic effects of change that launched it was tacitly attempted in order to establish stable conditions to develop the consensus. This was, in fact, the technique of human survival dominating to some extent individualistic bell-curve trends. Inotherwords there was an intellectual process carried out by which an "adaptive consensus" was reached—a sought condition of stability in a chaotic world. But trying to determine that stable condition did in fact create the very conditions that characterize the Dark Ages: Dissention over which direction the core civilization should be pointed became ferocious. As the nobility and clergy tried on one hand to persuade royalty to their point of view or on the other to influence the lower classes to support their self-serving cause, they undermined and kept undetermined this tacit drive for stability.

This phase—the so-called Dark Ages—was really the first reaction to a nascent realization of a greater world beyond the previous world states. It was also a reduction of view into localization as the great world states before were unable to prevent disintegration and chaos. Properly called an Age of Adjustment, this phase marks a retreat from the complexity that a sudden expansion of the already vast world states would incur. All aspects of civilization were characterized by a retreat behind defensive walls, both physically and socially. Retreat on the environment was one of these defensive factors. There was a great increase on reliance on the new one-god religions, since the old pantheisms failed to stop the depredations of disease, natural disasters and human whim. The collapse of the world states was seen as the weakening of an already incapable overseeing governmental organization's ability to control the environment to the advantage of large numbers of people. Attempts to physically control the environment were minimized as reliance on religion was seen as a means to "muddle through", sort of keeping a stiff upper lip so as to weather any storm. Thus there was a return of acquiescence to environmental conditions—yet long gone was the connection to nature that could have made surrendering to nature palatable—religion was the substitute.

In the early part of this phase, religion was the dominant factor in shaping civilization—it influenced education, philosophy, government, business; in short it touched almost all of society. Doing this was an attempt to establish a unity of belief better developed than that of the Secular/Clerical phase in order to restore the presumed peace and order of the great world states. At times, especially in Europe, extreme measures were taken in order to do this. At first was the use of excommunication to force compliance with Church principles. There were also rewards of dispensations for those championing Church principles. Later, as heresy seemed quite recalcitrant, use of the auto-da-fe became common, and finally the Inquisition was institutionalized. Christianity was thrust out of its philosophical debates and fundamentalist doldrums fully into the political arena, donning the armor of a male-dominated warrior religion. The political ramifications of this move drew religion into a maelstrom that to this day it has trouble dealing with. It did not take long for it to become both master and slave within the tumultuous political changes that characterized this phase. And as a further challenge it soon had an adversary, for the world's first true male-dominated warrior religion, Mohammedanism, burst upon the scene. Now Christianity, still developing its political "enforcement" arm of male-dominated warriorism, was confronted with a ready—if not fanatic—warrior enforced dominator with slowly evolving political capabilities. Their relationship comes to a head at the end of this phase.

With the triumph of these warrior Male/Father God religions, there was a return to distinct roles. In keeping with the order and organization sought for society, such role establishment attempted to simplify a once complex society to make organization easier. In many cases laws were enacted that institutionalized these roles, making distinct those things one or more people, male and/or female could or could not do.

This categorization fit right in with economic development of the time, and was reflected by changes in the educational system. A parochialism became the primary focus of society, especially in Europe, all of the grand designs of the world state were abandoned. Subconsciously, however, the concept of peace within a great world state became a fantasy though somewhat yearned for. For the most part, education was abandoned. Despite the establishment of schools by Charlemagne and other tentative steps taken elsewhere, education remained limited to the very few. As local industries prevailed, their needs were met by apprenticeship. Categorization aided the bourgeoisie, for they began at this time their long march to the influential position they enjoy today. They were the main ingredient, especially in Europe, for laying the foundations of today's modern economy at this time. At first, early in this phase, trade faltered but quickly revived. It then began to grow, along with the growth of industry—aided by the specialization of tasks at this time—that created interregional contacts that were mostly independent of governmental control. This widening reach resumed the pressures of intrusive change that ended the last phase. These pressures had changed, however, for now they were not only intellectual but economic, whereas the previous time was through physical pressure that forced intellectual change. As mentioned before, in Europe this balkanization that produced parochialistic societies, competing economies and a sense of local self-sufficiency shaped a civilization into something somewhat different from the other great centers in India and China. The socalled "European Ethic" that came to dominate the world was born.

Generally, this phase was racked with conflict in which the deciding factor was who was to rule society. With all of its wars and turmoil, it was not a chaotic era, for there was still adherence to the core principles of civilization: The acceptance of monarchial rule, the sanctity of religion and a general agreement on the "categorization" of society's members. It was an age of "retrenchment", an attempt to find shelter against a more interrelated world. Many rulers and intellectuals recognized this wider world but they were handcuffed by the great numbers of uneducated farmers, serfs and other laborers whose world was religion, having very little if any interest much beyond their immediate community. They were also handcuffed by bourgeois parochialism, the base of whose entrepreneurships would be challenged by an expanding—changing—world. From the first, as the great world governments crashed, there was a drive to reestablish their wide order and regularity. But the world had opened, and the gradually increasing influx of intrusive change prevented any easy solution. In China, government dominated, and being itself in turmoil prevented any progress toward coalescence until the next phase. The same in India except there religion ruled as regional government was unimportant for the fatalistic appearing idea that peace was individual and internal prevailed. In Europe, by the time Rome collapsed, the Church, having had four centuries of existence under imperial rule, had itself developed an organization very similar to the old order. It was thus able to step in and assume the duties of government that had suddenly collapsed. After all, for as long as anyone could remember, Rome had been the center of the "world" and now here was the Roman Church already the "Official Religion" after the Council of Nicaea assuming responsibility, sort of a tacit legitimacy to "take over".

But being the people's conscience and administering a society are two different things, and soon the Church found itself embroiled in the very controversies it abjured. It both used and was used by politicians to further various political gains. It was accused of corruption and influence peddling. Buffeted by these stresses, the Church began to look outward, to try to change the world outside Europe's sphere in order to stem the tide of alien ideas that fomented the troubles. As the Church was increasingly losing its relevance as governmental administrator, town and city governments came to the fore. This was the beginning of the European Ethic that was soon to dominate world history. For the towns could try to remain aloof from the Byzantine politics that racked Europe, relying on the wealth (sort of a symbiotic relationship) brought in by an increasingly influential bourgeoisie. At first, however, the bourgeoisie were not as involved in politics as were the nobility and clergy, relying instead on the power of their wealth to control local conditions. In the early stages of this phase, they kept to "doing their business", along with scientists and philosophers—the one establishing commercial strength, the other sorting out the growing tide of information, ideas and criticism flooding in from a rapidly widening world.

Toward the latter half of this phase, the power of all three clergy, nobility and bourgeoisie—had grown to considerable levels. Bourgeoisie power and influence had been gained from their entrepreneurships taking advantage of the commercialism of widening trade networks. Noble and clerical power was agricultural, gained on the backs of peasant farmers working the lands of their estates. Along with this rising power were increasingly vicious conflicts among them. Each was trying to assert their "rightness", trying to establish primacy. Usually, it was the clergy and nobility, supported off their backs, forced the peasantry into a precarious life. Trying to maintain control over these sometimes discordant forces was the monarchy, usually supportive of the peasant class to prevent them being bled into destitution by the Second Estate. This was a difficult task, and many were the monarchs drawn in by the entangled politics of the time just in trying to keep their country together with a functioning economy. For steering a survivable course while adhering to the then current rules of throne inheritance and alliance by marriage was a perilous business as bell curve positions among the Second Estate were beginning to stray. Most striking evidence of rulers being drawn into the fray was a movement that began the next phase, the Crusades.

This next phase, the fifth, is called **Secular I**. In Europe it covers the period from the Crusades, through the Renaissance and into Colonialism. China in this period was ruled by the Yuan, Ming and Ch'ing dynasties. India was taken over by Moslem rulers, the Moguls, who were later supplanted by the British. It was a period of extensive ongoing intrusive change that never allowed a society to relax—to develop its set. For change accelerated all through this phase; new ideas, new inventions, new ways of interpreting the world, were all accumulating in a great onrushing snowball that refused to let a society stop and rest. For now change was both internal and external: Internally there was a reaction to the previous breakdown period to bring wider areas into more singular views. This in order to keep out, or at least slow down to a manageable rate, change so that control of society could be simplified. It was an attempt to organize management of society and try to control change so as not to upset an established norm. But this was impossible due to two related reasons. Change was also external in its source; as the Crusades advanced they brought knowledge of a much wider, more complex world home that began to undermine accepted societal norms. Similarly the travels of Marco Polo, Fa-hsien, Zemarchos and others did the same. Different ideas and new products were spreading from a widening net of trade. At home, these experiences were sparking curiosity about the world; the development of scientific method began. Development of breaking out of the professed status quo of "normalcy" began as music, art and philosophy began experimenting in untried areas. Efficiencies of manufacturing's nascent industries spurred technological advancement. All of these intruded a level of change far more profound than had ever been experienced before. Now change fed upon itself, altering conditions that necessitated change in order to cope with it. A progression of advancing change was set in motion that has continued to this day.

Mankind's relation with his environment did not change much until the end of this phase. By that time the knowledge accumulated by science in its exploration of the world had discovered the true cause of disease. Attempts at control were begun also as science, having begun to dispel the long accepted beliefs based on folk and religious superstition, was elucidating the facts about our anatomy, why things occurred in the world and the nature of our universe. The environment eventually became "controllable" to a much greater extent than ever before. By the time of the Industrial Revolution it became merely a source from which the raw materials of industry were acquired. Science had yet to uncover how intimately related to his environment mankind was. Toward the end of this phase, being fueled at first by the competitiveness of the European Ethic, then later adding industrialism, provided Europe with a means to exploit the environment far more efficiently that had ever been seen before. These interrelated three gave Europe an advantage over the rest of the world's societies that allowed her worldwide expansion to succeed.

Though religion was defeated during this phase, ending its role as a significant player in the management and administration of society, its significance remained among those unable to keep up with the changing conditions. As economic growth included greater numbers of people in the fate of their society—as the bell curve positions of greater and greater numbers of people began to find independent positions— as the persistence of change seemed to never allow the calmness of a steady state, religion remained as the focus of being: An unchanging truth that became an anchor for many to "weather the storm", so to speak. But the cynical aspect of religion continued as it has since mankind's earliest history; used as a tool by royalty, nobility or the bourgeoisie to try to influence the population into supporting a certain political point of view or the old religion based core of civilization. "Warriorism" became justified as European colonialism spread around the world. The European nations justified their militant Christianity at first to secure raw material sources and trade privileges. Moreso though later, when colonial holdings became pawns in the international politics among the European nations themselves, did efforts to convert native populations accelerate. For Christianization was thought to make it easier to bring people into compliance with the European way of doing things. So from the Crusades, to African slavery, Chinese spheres of influence to native American slaughter—and of course throughout this phase, Jewish pogroms—the rest of the world was caught up in the playout of the competitiveness of the European ethic.

With religion's defeat, this phase marks the rise of philosophy, for it was better able to assimilate the great increase in knowledge and technological advances that took place in its last few centuries. Religion found itself enmeshed in the problem of maintaining relevance of instruction it used to try to bring order during the previous phase. Its orientation to the post bronze-age, early iron-age agricultural world of its creation upon which its foundation was based could not be altered in any significant way without jeopardizing its efficacy. It was increasingly limited to matters of the soul and the moral composure of both the individual and society. It found less of a voice in the flood of ideas that characterized the Renaissance, Enlightenment and especially Industrial periods that ended this phase. For along with these arose ideas of individualism and freedom from religion's control.

This phase saw a tremendous growth and alteration of education. Throughout most of it, the educational system for most people remained the same; apprenticeship for those lucky enough to gain a position. Since it took most of the population throughout most of this phase to produce food—including feeding the animals that provided not only meat but power—the "way of doing things" remained much the same century to century. Education under these conditions was not really a concern, for farming was a peasant occupation and methods were carried on within the family, generation to generation. The great industrial farming states of the Secular/Clerical phase, disintegrated during the breakdown phase, were now great baronial estates worked by peasants who were indentured to the support of the noble. But education did realize tremendous growth. The rapid spread of increasing world-wide trade brought more than just goods, it maintained an influx of ideas; mores, religious and philosophical thought, and general expansion of the world view. The competitiveness of Europe was only augmented by this—a rising curiosity about the world, about economics, about humankind, about history—was manifest. Greek and Roman historiography, philosophy, geography, poetry and literature were rediscovered. Education, still confined largely to the upper classes—and to rising numbers of the bourgeoisie—began to explore the meaning of life, of existence and to establish the "rightness" of the European viewpoint. In the spirit of European competitiveness, however, philosophy separated from religion, and science began to develop an inductive methodology, while the bourgeoisie were as yet to capitalize on what this would mean for them. There was wide-spread development of colleges and universities with their emphasis on the Greek and Roman classics. But the wideranging differences that world-wide contacts were bringing—forces of intrusive change—were at first intoxicating. It did not take long, however, for a change in focus to develop. Intrusive change demands the challenge to be met. Explanations must be provided, and old classics couldn't deliver reasons and explanations for new conceptions and discoveries. By the dawn of the Industrial Revolution, the aggregate of human knowledge had grown considerably. From Copernicus, Galileo and Gutenberg, the pace of technological and scientific knowledge acquisition began an acceleration that continues today. Though moveable type printing had been in use long before this time in China, it found more fertile ground in the competitiveness of Europe. It spread quickly, and with it the chronicling of the rising pace of knowledge growth—a condition in itself that contributed to intrusive change and spurred further inquiry. As technological advancement rushed forward, eventually developing into the Industrial Revolution, educational curricula were forced to diversify; more specialization began to be stressed. The importance of education transitioned from giving society classics-trained generalists to technical and scientific-trained specialists. (Though generalists never completely disappeared, such as some philosophers and the author of this book.) For the first time educational focus began anticipating the future—what should be, and how can that be achieved with the present state of scientific and technological knowledge. Unfortunately this change in focus began to outstrip the means of enabling the numbers of people necessary to comprehend society's growing complexity (generalism) which was to confound society in the next phase.

One of the greatest changes to occur during this phase was in the field of economics. The spread of explorers and traders to be followed by armies and clerics was spurred by the need to maintain trade connections—heretofore overland across Asia—blocked by the Moslem hegemony. Quickly the established agriculturally oriented system of serfdom with some slavery and cottage industry expanded, providing a foundation for the eventual development of industrialization. Spurred by wider-ranging trade, the European ethic transformed this into a quickly developing factory system. Guilds developed a measure of power. World-wide trade and the extension of European politics into the forces of colonialism saw the emergence of Mercantilism and the press to develop "spheres of influence" to guarantee trade and raw material privileges while at the same time trying to maintain a competitive advantage over rival states.

In the beginning of this phase European development wasn't much different from the rest of the world, with its civilization pretty much on par with the others. But the development of an economic system fairly free of governmental interference, coupled with the complex of technological and scientific developments, a rising factory system and more widely available knowledge in the form of books and newspapers, brought more and more of the common people into greater conversance with their rapidly developing world. Toward the end of this phase, this familiarity gave rise to monarchial decline and the development of more common, or elective governments.

The bourgeoisie also came into their own during this phase: Producing the arms of colonialism and its wars, their factories soon made much of scientific and technological development, aided by an abundant workforce easily accepting greater specialization in the system. The complexities and growing interrelationships of regional—and ultimately world—economics was not lost on some. Economists such as Smith, Dupont de Nemours and others began to develop economic theories describing what was happening in order to both understand and project into the future. But the past was not altogether abandoned. In a rapidly changing world in which positions don't seem to have any security, truths are looked for in a past that is presumed to have been "stable" or where "right and wrong" were clear and distinct. Such was the case with European Jews who, from confusing religious myth with fact, were largely denied being farmers, artisans or entrepreneurs. Since the dawn of Christianity, they were harassed, plundered and denied living like most other people. The Crusades were mostly funded by plundering Jewish homes and settlements. Consequently these people became "portable" entrepreneurs, adopting vocations they could take with them in an emergency. Banking was one of these. The rise of the new economic state was crippled in Spain and Italy, and among others to a lesser degree, when even this was denied them: They were expelled from Spain (1492) and placed in ghettoes in Italy.

In other places the past survived as autocratic rule kept an iron hand on national economy and/or the manipulation of public policy. Much of this was a response to colonial forces from Europe, for a powerful monarch was the only one capable of mustering enough ability to withstand the pressure. It was only Thailand, however, that managed to remain free of any colonial manipulation.

This phase, the fifth, was really a reaction to the fourth, but the continuous flow of intrusive change remained through both. For the most part, reaction to the change (from the outside) was internalized during the fourth and was externalized during the fifth. The situation was more frustrating during the fifth because the intrusive change came not only from the outside but was generated increasingly from the inside (scientific, technological, social, literary, etc.). Local differences due to European competitiveness assured similar developments of societies' general characteristics. The rise of nation states—expanding coalescence of local governmental or tribal areas—was an attempt to establish a common "base" to bring unity and order to the previous phase's perceived chaos. This rise followed that of the European ethic that had its roots in the previous phase. It was wrought not only from conditions outlined above but also was a reaction to warrior religions that gave it a particularly militaristic flavor. It was therefore a militaristic base that evolved, coupled with competitiveness set Europe on her drive toward the domination of world history. It was thought that from this base internal security could be achieved (so it was hoped) in order to address differences with adjoining states. But the very success of the European ethic denied the nation states' their desired ends. The steady rise of education, standards of living, information availability—not to exclude more widespread familiarity with the nobility—allowed more and more people of the lower classes to analyze, accept or question the status quo, or proposed status quo. As a broader spectrum of the population became more exposed to the intrusive change generated both internally and from wide ranging trade and colonialism, opinions began to diverge and challenges to both positions and opinions began to appear. This involvement of great numbers of people in the workings of their society and attempts to direct its fate led to an emergence of elective governments, first in England and Holland, then the United States and France. This meant that moving positions on society's bell curves, heretofore a "luxury" of the upper classes, now became ever more commonplace. There was a rise of bell curve position separation that goes on yet today. In some states the monarch was forced to assume greater autocratic power in order to maintain control and attenuate the intense conflict that grew between nobility and bourgeoisie—the landed class versus ever more economically powerful entrepreneurs/ capitalists. Additionally, there was a continuation from the previous phase, of the bourgeoisie joined by the religious establishment, resisting any of the changes shaped by intrusive change. Time, knowledge accumulation, governmental/societal and economic sophistication, along with the beginnings of psychological science increased the consensus' resistance to this historical obstructionism.

Competition among the European nation-states spread around the world, resulting in colonial empires whose members were themselves drawn into the conflicts. So many factors had now become relevant to shaping the consensus of a nation that it seemed chaos would prevail. The great capitalist bourgeoisie houses, the established church and a few autocratic hangers on—though preserving a semblance of order—prevented the normal evolution of the consensus. By the end of this phase two things became apparent: The directional stability that civilization's core tenets gave the consensus weakened, allowing a breakup into several consensi. The result of this was that great blocks of population adhered to a certain persuasion—be it economic, religious, militaristic, societal, etc; in an effort to find "safety" in a seemingly chaotic world. With these great opinion blocks, allowance for consensus evolution was curtailed and there was militant pressure to demand adherence to a point of view disallowing bell curve divergence. Unacknowledged among all groups was that the very core tenets of human society were beginning to be questioned. As if to force the consensus into a certain direction, these consensi, these opinion blocks, each pushed their point of view. By the end of this phase this became a process of information delivery in an attempt to sway popular opinion among a population largely unable to assimilate the changes of a fast-changing world. Widespread newspapers, the telegraph and telephone spread the word at unheard of speeds reaching the greatest number of people possible in a very short amount of time.

These were the conditions during the overlap between this phase and the next, the sixth. The Sixth phase is called the **Great Transition** that stands astride the end of the Fifth and beginning of the Seventh. The Sixth spans only a period of about two centuries; the period from the collapse of Napoleon's empire to the collapse of Russia's Communist empire. These two centuries were a Great Transition for it was during this time that science and technology rushed the future upon mankind. That rush was so fast that humanity was caught unaware. Meanwhile, the nation states, still trying to retain their independence and justify their relevancy, were being notified by events progressing from rapidly changing societies that their time may be limited. For societies were altering by gradually adopting a worldwide consensus, and cooperating in ways that were making the nation-states increasingly irrelevant.

The transition begins with the end of the Napoleonic empire, signalling the end of dreams of a great Roman Empire style World State. An air of uncertainty hung over the world as pre-Napoleonic forces tried to reassert themselves, reorganizing Europe the way it was before. But Napoleon had unleashed a new sense of "Europeanism" that could not be subjected to the old ways. Only the British empire, seeking to preserve itself, made a change that anticipated the future; it became a Commonwealth of Nations; an organization of nations.

But the nineteenth century was a century of tremendous scientific, technological and industrial development. A technology totally unheard of had descended upon societies still wrestling with their inertia from the last phase. These forces of the past met this future technology and the past was defeated each time: First was the United States' Civil War in which products of industrialism—new and more powerful armaments and weapons—overpowered the soldier resulting in great slaughter with a fearful efficiency. This was copied in the Franco-Prussian war of 1870. There were others, wars of disruption and the inability to accept the future: The Chinese monarchy, enervated by years of colonial "spheres of influence" and an imposed opium trade, was made irrelevant in wars with Russia and Japan (who, with Turkey, were the last of the autocracies). These wars and their aftermath foreshadowed the destructiveness capable of an organized nation state armed with the latest technological innovations.

But these last conflicts paled beside the final act of the past meeting the future technology: World War I burst upon a humanity—though somewhat nervous about the direction world affairs seemed to be going—that was fairly complacent, not too worried about any great change coming over their lives. World War I, however, **was** a bringer of tremendous change. It was the last gasp of autocracy (Russia— ended by revolution—Prussia, Austria-Hungary and Turkey) in resisting the accelerating thrashing out of bell-curve positions that was becoming world-wide: Expressed as independence movements of peoples, even those frustrated by living within a nation state.

Realization that the coming new order supersedes independently acting nation-states was stated by Theodore Roosevelt, Churchill and especially Woodrow Wilson. They voiced what many felt; that a new order was necessary as the world's events, economics and social structure was quickly extending beyond borders. The nation-states were losing the ability to be sole arbiters of their future. World War I's aftermath brought realization of how destructive technological development can be. There must be controls on states to keep this tremendous power in check. And so the League of Nations was born.

Establishing the League of Nations, however, was undermined by forces resistant to change who, at the forefront, were the bourgeoisie. The nineteenth century was their century: They rode a whirlwind of fabulously successful industrial advancements about which no elaboration is needed. The accumulated great amounts of wealth—wealth that gave them a great amount of political power. It was reminiscent of phase IV; governments were comfortable with allowing entrepreneurs to carry on, building the nation's economic stature. But government acquiescence was falling back on the past hoping to secure the future. When the United States opted not to join the League of Nations, forces were let loose that would soon make World War I look like a picnic. First, government became compliant to the bourgeoisie world view. Economic policies were followed that led to a severe world wide depression, made all the worse by large numbers of dependent urban dwellers who no longer worked on farms. Secondly, with the United States not a member, age-old hatreds between France and Germany were allowed free reign; France was able to force a heavy debilitating fine on Germany that so destroyed her economy that it became fertile ground for demagoguery. The League of Nations quickly fell apart, ending any attempt to forge a desperately needed new world order. The depression, however, destroyed the legitimacy of the bourgeoisie as directors of the affairs of government and the economy. Meanwhile, as if to prevent coming under bourgeoisie influence, Russia reconsolidated her old empire of the Czars as a Soviet Union organized as a rival of capitalism called communism.

The aftermath of this explosive situation was a war thought to have been never possible. World War II, in comparison with number I, was of gigantic proportions, especially after the United States became involved. This was the first war in which technology began to address survival of the fighting man, though losses were still high. This war, like no other, affected the future far more than has yet to be realized. It began as a massive headlong rush of intrusive change of a new type, a globally oriented change, that upset a world still not adjusted to the interregional changes that brought on the Great Transition. The last quarter of this phase was rife with warfare as humanity struggled with digesting this new order. China returned to autocracy—calling in communism—for two reasons; to save herself from self-destruction that was occurring under the republic, and to strengthen her perimeter (control of Tibet and Mongolia) as defense against a resurgent Soviet Union and independent India. Minorities called for a return to the past seen comparably as stability and order. Yet there was a sense about this—a subconsciousness of the Spirit—among most of humanity: It sounds good, returning to the old religion, the old government, the old (simpler) economics, the old family "values", yet these ring hollow. The consensus needs a satisfactory foundation upon which to rest.

Before this phase, the world was moving along at a more or less steady but incremental rate of advancement. The ongoing intrusive change was enough to keep things unstable to the point where humanity became inured to the change and called it instead "history". Milestones of change were noted, that is, when the accumulation of change became noticeable, and were named "counter reformation", or "renaissance', or "enlightenment". Even the beginning of the sixteenth century was considered the beginning of "modern" history. But all this seemingly orderly procession was destroyed by the Great Transition. Everything was thrown into disorder. Let us see how.

The nineteenth century was the industrial century. It was an era of a coal-fired, steam-driven, society with smokestacks and waste pipes. There was wholesale acquisition of raw materials as science and technology moved quickly in devising new uses, new methods and new inventions to feed the frenzy. Yet in its workings, science began to stumble upon the interrelationships that exist between mankind and the rest of nature. The last half of this phase saw a rise in environmental awareness, efforts to understand and not disrupt ecological orders. Additionally, as the world's population mushroomed and consumerism became the engine of economics, realization that the world's resources were limited became evident. The hell-bent use of resources as if there were no tomorrow started giving way to resource recycling and better use planning.

Religion had died in the previous phase. Taking advantage of the thoroughgoing disruption of this, the Great Transition, however, it became one of those minorities that called for a return to the presumed stability, simplicity and order of the past. A religious orientation was seen as an ordered shelter providing a stable life in what appeared to be a chaotic world. The unease that gripped the potential consensus, however, limited this view to minorities among all the religions. Those that would make the consensus sensed that more to a solution than this was required.

One of the contributors to the Great Transition, and the end of phase V, was education. Development of colleges and universities mush-roomed in order to address the tremendous change this phase was reflecting—a transition into the next. A huge demand had to be satis-fied for those capable of understanding current situations, capable of continuing the ongoing development of science and technology and capable of carrying out the new tasks necessary to function within a society of increasing complexity. Education's focus became oriented more and more toward specialization. A myriad of specialties, specifi-cally organizational and administrative, to coordinate the interrelationships among them all. This was a harbinger of the future; a highly scientific and technological world that had no references to the old religions, the old ethnicities and the old social mores. Even here in education there were minorities crying out to return to the val-ues of the past and not dehumanize life by ignoring them. They wanted education to teach ethnic histories, religious "success", ethics based on the past, for it was felt that without remembering these aspects of our ancestry, our future will have no heart. But the scien-tific/technological world of this phase caught up with education. As the information retrieval and supply system became available world-wide, as industrial machinery became more efficient—increasingly computer controlled—education began wondering just what **should** be taught in our schools, colleges and universities? Indeed, there were questions of **what** should be taught, and **how** should it be taught! The Great Transition was displaying a possible future of constant change that education was unable to prepare for.

One of the most telling aspects of this phase was the break-down of social structure. The first three quarters of this phase was characterized by rigid family structures and "places" for everyone in society. The last quarter, however, saw an expansion of freedom, a liberalization that flourished in only a few generations. Never has such profound change worked its way through a civilization so quickly. Several things made this possible; the birth control pill, demands by women to be treated as equals with men, relationships becoming more important than rigid family structures, and psychology becoming the means by which relationships are understood. Another factor was the overwhelming world-wide spread of information storage, retrieval and access. This phase saw the rate of information exchange sky-rocket—from the telegraph to satellite connected computers—making political borders only physical restraints. Idea exchanges among individuals was occurring world-wide, creating a forum for questioning various status quos and consensus' positions. Those countries that tried to hang on to the past by restricting or preventing this exchange, found it tough going.

Probably the least understood by most but which also experienced a tremendous change was the field of economics. Though the reality of an integrated world economy became evident with the counter-blockades of England and Napoleon, phase VI was a watershed. As the industrial juggernaut consumed the world, to be followed by consumerism and the blurring of political boundaries, economics lost its Smithian simplicity, maturing beyond post-Keynesian concepts. The two world wars dictated the future of the world's economy. It became one where national currencies are traded like stock on exchanges, where their value is dependent upon their nation's economic policies. Government spending and taxation are coordinated to modulate currency value which is determined by its "velocity". No longer is money backed by gold or some other finite medium. Now the determination was by how frequently it changes hands (its "velocity") in relation to national production and consumption rates. Since these rates were contingent upon a free exchange of goods, services and ideas, any nation state that resisted integration into this new economic order found itself both struggling to maintain parity and a source of difficulty for all others.

From the Napoleonic wars to World War I the nation states were increasingly forced into cooperative ventures that went far beyond treaties of joint support or common interests. This meant they must become more inclusive and accept their collective will expressed through an overseeing organization. Such was the aim of the League of Nations. But millennia of jealously guarded national economic control raised its hand, leading to the recession that spawned World War II forcing the new economics onto a largely unwilling world. For the new economic order was part of that future world prepared by the Great Transition: A world made borderless by rapid information exchange and interdependent economic relationships that depended on flexible national economic management. It was this necessary flexibility that dictated the demise of the rigid Communist systems. Capitalism was also dying, as the Great Transition has pointed the world toward some form of managed economy.

No greater change ever befell mankind than that of the Great Transition. The rampant industrialism that started as this phase began seemed to take on a life of its own. Its systemization, its management demands and its press for ever greater efficiency with reduction of manpower use spawned a most thoroughgoing technological revolution. The result of all this, however, was a humanity left at sea. Mankind's world had been so thoroughly disrupted that certainty was gone and direction toward the future was unconvincing. The next phase, the Seventh, was well underway by this time.

The Seventh phase is called **Secular II**. Its beginning coincides with the start of the 20th century while its end lies sometime in the future. This phase can be called the "post-colonial" while some would say Modern, yet it is a tumultuous phase of human readjustment to the completely different world ushered in by the Great Transition. Its length will be determined by mankind, for it is the last phase of our Dark Age. Only he can determine how quickly he will adopt the new, necessary and inevitable global singular civilization laid out by the Great Transition. For this is a phase of great potential, the deciding moment that will cast the forming of the species homo sapiens sapiens. It will be the era in which mankind determines the manner in which he decides to exist—in order or in chaos.

The millennia long ordeal of intrusive change reaches its climax, becoming pandemic. Its rampant thoroughness touches all parts of human civilization. It is overwhelming. Constant change now becomes normal, it becomes the status quo. Such a state of constant change—or that society created by these conditions—is extremely disruptive. Many of these ongoing changes are caused by human choices, their disruption is decried but no solutions are forthcoming, for solutions mean more change. What is most disruptive is that all things are being questioned, including the very core of civilization. No longer is mankind allowed to slip back onto his old constants of good/bad, male/female, family, work/live, religion/civilization, etc. Although many, individuals and consensi, because of the uncertainess of the future this disruption creates, do try to revive these old concepts. A certain militancy arises by some as they try to end change and return to a stable world.

The meteoric rise of scientific knowledge about our world during the Great Transition brought about another completely new situation: The environment was now almost wholly dominated by mankind. Wide-spread destruction transcends the boundaries of the nation-states: As toxic chemicals are weather or aquifer born, as one activity harms the welfare of another activity, the harmful side effects of massive industry and of convenience consumerism can no longer just be "put out of the way". Population pressures, feeding rising consumerism, drive both industry and government to minimize harmful side-effects so as not to reduce the availability of convenient consumerism. Along with this are popular notions of environmental simplicity, that solutions are simple, solvable and therefore not harmful to the system. There is the refusal by most to recognize the pervasiveness and importance of environmental relationships. The assuagement of human needs, though felt to be important, is nonetheless uncertain from fears that the ongoing widespread destruction should be addressed. Environmental problems seem to continue, to worsen, as the ability of government to regulate mankind's relationship with the environment recedes. This because as environmental knowledge increased and became more complex, resultant governmental regulation began to be perceived as working at cross purposes. But a system that lives off the environment without consideration of that environment cannot long survive. Just as societies evolved as a synthesis of religion, environmental necessities and symbiotically tailored social laws, so too has the modern industrial/technological state. As with the development of the European dynamic, development of the modern industrial/technological system has seen religion pushed into the background and systematic environmental exploitation increase dramatically. This system was acceptable when its fruits accrued to the few ruling nations while the majority of the world's people remained agricultural. But as industrialization and the fruits of a modern economy spread throughout all of the world—ie; the rise of "consumerism"—the system is not geared to this condition. One could muse that the system is based upon exploitation of both labor and the environment. Indeed, when an increasing percentage of population no longer what to be "exploited" and the environmental strains that this exploitation is necessarily revealing, demand for change is presented. A whole new environmental relationship is being called for that present day stop-gap measures do not adequately address: The drive for fuel efficiency only delays the economic problems that will arise when those finite resources come into short supply. The big push for recycling is commendable but few things are truly recycled: Glass, aluminum, copper and steel are the only ones. The rest, plastic, paper, wood, uranium, chrome, etc, are used once, sometimes transformed into something else—such as plastic bottles into insulation—as a final state. This still constitutes the using up of materials. Those civilizations that understood living within the environment, which also meant recognizing that other species have rights of domain, have been and are being overwhelmed by those that don't. So in this final phase of our long Dark Age, a whole new environmental order is being called for, an order that presents mankind with two choices: Humanity must once again live in complete harmony with his planet if he is to escape the cycles of history and achieve some level of stasis. Or he must be completely separated from it.

Religion, and its justification of having provided the foundation upon which societies have been built are being challenged. Now in the last stage of our long Dark Age, the traditions of established social mores and conventions are being broken by the centrifugal forces of change. The omniscience of information communication has made people world-wide aware of things going on everywhere. Ideas that have never been brought to open discussion—or at least so widely considered—are now exerting the most profound pressures of change on society world-wide. This has fractionated religion more than usual. Individual expression is leading religious thought onto many different paths. A modern version of Hellenistic society exists, in which spiritualism and various cult beliefs become as legitimate as the old line religions. This is a search for religious efficacy in a world wherein international events, science, technology, medicine psychology and other forces of intrusive change are reducing religious faith to an anachronism. But the forces of the past aren't easily extinguished; they raise a formidable resistance to this demand for change. A demand that is largely ignored in order to protect the Spirit from not having a base upon which to establish a reason for being. So there are demands to return to religion's rule to restore morality, community, ethics, etc. A search for beginning begins; to find that religious expression that can bring order to chaos. In this phase, however, where the demands of intrusive change have become normalcy, this religious desire for order (and a new basis of being) can't be achieved until it addresses the future.

In this phase, education is in limbo. Only scientific and technological learning continue, for they will change the least as the world of the future evolves. Throughout the centuries, education had been attuned to the consensus. It was one of the ties that linked generations into maintaining civilization. As positions of the consensus's changed, so too did the orientation of education. By the Great Transition it had become highly specialized, for education's importance had changed. It became the mechanism that prepared various people for highly specialized tasks rather than producing objective people with a broad world view. This was successful, too, for the economy and social conditions produced by the scientific/technological/industrial state was due largely to large numbers of specialized workers. Further it was successful because the whole thrust of the system was to ease the burdens of labor so more leisure time would be available for all. So during this phase education is training many for tasks that fewer need. With the absence of a large enough population with a broad world view, too many lack the "big picture" and feed the breakup of the consensus. Education is enervated, for it no longer knows what to teach: When the jobs for which it prepares its students no longer exist, or are in such low demand, what to do? Additionally, the information explosion has overwhelmed education. There doesn't seem to be enough time in a lifetime to become somewhat conversant with it all, let alone time spent in school. In this phase as society breaks down, as the many interrelated tasks of the industrial/technological society dwindle—and along with them the modern society's meaning of existence—education finds itself in another field. For along with a fractionating society, there is a breakup of family structure. It too is being swept along in the uncertainty of what is to be in the future. Meanwhile, the educational establishment begins to be de facto parents, as it tries to shape the task of facing the future with other organizations suffering from the disintegration: Religion, business, government, charities, etc.

Even the world's economy, which was a major player in the Great Transition, was finding itself affected by the troubles of this phase. It continued what was begun during the Great Transition: Converting from industrialism to a technocracy. Technocracy, however, is unfamiliar, proposing an uncertain future. During the conversion, which marks this phase, there is a break-down of economic order: After the contest between Capitalism—a market/consumer—and Communism—or planned economic orders—was decided in favor of Capitalism, there now remained the problem of determining how it can best serve the future population. The past again raises its hand, because the triumph of a market/consumer economy is the triumph of the bourgeoisie. They had raised advertising to an art form fully utilizing the new science of psychology in sustaining the market economy. Now they renew the anti-government fervor that has characterized their ilk since the Second Phase. Blaming government and its social programs as the reasons for this phase's confusion, they loudly discredit the very social developments that made the modern economy from which they has greatly benefitted possible. Ever the frustrated "nobility", they aim to free themselves from government taxes and regulations for their own gain. Taking advantage of moribund education exacerbates the situation. Their call to return to the "stability" of the past—let business run business, let religion guide society—is but another of the organizations trying to reaffirm the past to rid society of this phase's confusion. With computerization and cybernation, however, the old standards of working at a job to earn a living—pay your own way—is being called into question. The labor intensive industries that provided high incomes for great numbers of people, thereby fueling today's post-Keynesian economy have been largely replaced by machinery—computer run machinery. From miners to manufactures, machinists to engineers, even operators of trains, planes and ships, are becoming relegated to the simplified task of just operation, most of it being automated. The need for high income/high risk positions are diminishing. How is an economic system based upon great numbers of people with high incomes that fuel that system survive when the vast majority of people no longer have those high incomes?

The products of industrialism and technology, made possible by hyperspecialization and the disappearance of generalists, act to destroy that system that created them. Manufacturing ability has become so sophisticated and automatic it isn't necessary for the workers to be highly skilled nor highly paid. How can an economic system that was based upon a ratio of humans looking upon vast areas of expansion and apparent unlimited opportunity survive when a huge population faces shrinking expansion and increasingly limited opportunities? A most profound change is being thrust upon an economic system that is not geared to taking care of population numbers far beyond what was ever imagined. Its inability to provide for the security and wellbeing of today's huge population is bringing upon it the same centrifugal forces that are breaking up the consensus. The economy will be unable to regulate dropouts as they spread a rise in small entrepreneurships. There will be, however, a concentration of wealth and of "governmental" control in the hands of large businesses instigating a fundamental change in civilization: The long standard relationship of government separate from but working with the economy—that gave rise to the European dynamic—now will be supplemented by a melding of the two into a corporate government. Large, global businesses begin taking over operation of civilization just as the Roman Church did after the collapse of Rome: They are the only organized and disciplined entities capable of doing so. Global trade in information exchange lays the foundation for ending the Dark Age: A whole new economic order is being called for that will assure the health, welfare and sustenance of all of its citizens in a way completely different from any that have gone before. The time it takes to change or evolve into this system, which will occur during this phase, will depend on how willingly people are to modify their bell-curve positions. As we have seen, willful movement of bell-curve position is resisted quite strongly. Especially with economics; evolution is very slow since self interests are at stake.

Perhaps most disrupted by the Great Transition was the social state. The spread of industrialism and technology brought with it a sense of self-control over individual lives, a greater liberalism began to emerge. This self-control was translated into local control and a consequent drive for popular government—in some cases a push for democracy. The influx of a great variable world, just as during the Fourth Phase, caused a great wandering of bell curve positions: Some tried new things, some reacted against it. The inability of government to find a way to apply a steadying hand (except those opting for dictatorial control) made it seem ineffectual. The now normal state of change was seen as disintegration, leading toward chaos unless "something is done". The fabric of society was perceived as breaking down. People tried to form consensi as they tried to recapture the "stability" of the past by aligning with a religion, an ethnicity, an economic philosophy, etc. This descent into neotribalism meant small groups were trying to find meaning because society as a whole seemed unsure of its meaning, even its form. The uncertainty of the future in an atmosphere of continuous change created fear that drove the small consensi into hardening their positions. Governments began to fragment, especially the democracies, into smaller governmental units (gated communities, closed borders, etc). This struggle saw the emergence of other consensi intertwined among the others as people struggled to find meaning: They championed political correctness; religion, ethnicity; social, cultural and/or lingual "assurances"—as positions from which society should base the core of its revitalization. The world is descending into a state of "society—not society" in which there are attempts to uphold the old core foundations yet they are challenged by the double edged sword of change being normalcy and the ubiquitousness of information storage and retrieval. Fear of the future unknown because of ongoing change feeds some militancy of various positions. But now the core itself, the very essence of mankind's civilization is being challenged. This has never before happened. The Great Transition telegraphed the message that mankind has truly entered a new era, and that he cannot live in parochial societies separated from each other either socially, economically, environmentally or by political boundaries.

The Great Transition so completely undermined the basic tenets of human existence that the two phases, the one before and the one after, are almost alien to each other. Never since mankind chose to become agricultural instead of hunter-gatherers has such a change made its way across his societies. That change, however, was slow, for it was an evolution that allowed compensating adjustments of bell curves. This change, on the other hand, is rapid, very rapid by historical standards. For the bell curve changes of position are not allowed their normal evolutionary alteration. There is much resistance to the dawning global economy, society and the mind boggling concept that all things are related. With the explosion of information availability, any action by any entity, from individual to nation state and its reaction become measured by their effects on other people, nations, economies, environments, religions, etc. So governments struggle to find a way to make themselves more representative of their people. Their people sense this as an attempt to attenuate their growing separateness to provide forms for status-quo coalescence in an attempt to orchestrate the bell curves. But how to orchestrate the bell curves revives the old past versus future conflict. Those seeking to keep the past become "conservative", trying to reinforce past practices to justify their validity—because "they worked". Laws are passed to try to both consolidate past practices and to establish a "status-quo", in order to arrest society's fractionation. Such attempts to retain past practices only alienates others. There is a rejection of government, economy, education, religion, etc. So as consternation and frustration builds over the apparent unsolvability of the breakdown characterizing this phase, due to growing awareness of all things being relative to everything else, a search for a new beginning gets underway. The basis for a new civilization must be established. What the Great Transition began is what must be thrashed out in this penultimate phase of mankind's history: No longer is the parochialism of regional consensi acceptable—the basis of the new and future civilization must be world wide: There are great conflicts underway, one being that we must decide what constitutes a family. If family is the basis for passing acculturation to the children, then all must be similar to become a working group, or community. We must decide what our religion will be, what language we're going to use, what our money is going to be called and what constitutes justice. We must accept the fact that gender differences and sexuality are genetically controlled, so too are body shape, skin, hair and eye color—states we must celebrate as the variety of mankind, for our future civilization is one that may seem monotonous today. Keeping in mind that civilization can only exist when religion, society, economy and relationship with the environment are interrelated, the future civilization that follows this phase can only be when this occurs. Political parties will disappear as they are inherently parochial and cannot address the issues of a fully integrated world economy and society. It will be a world-wide civilization of a large human population cooperating within and existing under the guidance of the newest science of psychology. The nation-states will become but administrative districts as the world itself becomes one nation. This phase will end as this occurs, for the fully integrated world will thus become a nation-world, and mankind will finally be able to begin his future.

CHAPTER 7

Rising Out of the Dark Age

Predicting the future is at best a risky business with absolutely no certainty of the outcome. There are several factors, however, that can perhaps provide a guide toward a reasonable assumption of what our world will be like at the end of the present phase. Because of the scientific, industrial, technological and information availability that exploded into history during the Great Transition, we know that the process of evolving toward the end of our present phase will be far more rapid than has been historical development before. Clues to the shape of our future society lie in the very mechanism of evolution itself. Remember that the reason for evolution is to realize security for the cell. Since mankind's evolution changed from physical to social, the shape of his nation-world will directly reflect this achievement of cellular security.

First, a recapitulation. When mankind separated himself from nature, deciding to try to be free of natural cycles and occurrences, not only did his evolutionary method change from physical to social, but his long dark age began. Called "dark" for convenience, it was really a long period of readjustment to determine the proportions of separate and one-with. Or, how much of the Panessence, that interconnector of individuals of each species, was he to be cognizant of? Actually not much, for the Panessence is of the soul, which requires subservience to the so-called "Laws" or "Ways of Nature". So his Spirit was left to determine his essence, mankind's purpose of being. This took a whole new direction, for Spirit is not connected to the Soul, and was free to invent. So this Spirit displayed its irrepressibility as evidenced by the steady accelerating development of technology, science and culture. These were oriented on the use of nature for reference and raw materials. For Spirit, without the connection to nature enjoyed by soul, sought to force nature to conform to its demands. Nature was to be exploited, and this exploitation enabled humankind to develop science, technology and his cultures whose forms were related to the environment in which they arose. Growth of humanity's cultures, along with their science and technology, was led by his religions as they also evolved into newer forms to enable him to face evolving but uncertain futures.

This was done by recasting the known in futuristic terms so that the unknown could be approached. So animism presented the known in terms of familiar spirits that enabled mankind to function in nature as a being separated from nature. This was the "Mother Earth" religion; animistic spirits or anthropomorphic characterizations that both reflected and recognized the earth's trappings as fellow spiritual companions. As his world expanded, conflicts with different animistic spirits for the same things had to be resolved. The earth itself became the foundation connecting animistic systems. Earth, the "mother" of all life, became represented as a Mother Goddess who represented fertility and reproduction—a locus that legitimized all the other animistic spirits. Conflicts continued, and they had to be resolved. The only way was by upgrading animistic spirits to a more remote pantheon. These gods/goddesses had a generic connection with the old animism—god of the sea, of forest, of the sky, of wind, etc: The earth-oriented Mother Goddess that helped mankind to understand and cooperate with nature was replaced by a pantheon of gods and goddesses who now controlled nature. Cooperation was replaced by propitiation if mankind was to be able to assure his existence. Just as cooperation among the members of these new pantheons was necessary for a secure world. For now the locus of Mother Goddess has been replaced by a somewhat sexually balanced group. A group slightly male dominated—perhaps to provide needed strength in a rising tide of warfare over trade, religious disputes and geographical advantage. These new pantheons were far more powerful that the more local animistic systems, and so could extend a singular system over a much wider area. In this way civilization could expand far beyond tribal limitations. As it did, however, soon even these pantheons had localized limitations, and a new spiritual concept had to be devised that allowed the understanding of an even greater world. The direct spiritual connection of mankind with his environment had to become even more comprehensive. Now thinking in terms of "the world", one-god religions that included all of the old animistic concepts under the umbrella of "part of that created by god", or manifestations of the spirit of god, evolved. By making the environment even more remote from any direct spiritual connection with humanity enabled mankind to range far and wide, all under the aegis of a "universal" god. These One gods were male "Father Gods", necessary to provide the strength required to dominate both nature and other societies for trade advantages and economic survival. Propitiation was still required in order to remain in these new Father, or "warrior", god's good graces. This turmoil of transition between the pantheons and spread of the one-god, one-world religions occurred during phase three. It had its beginnings in the Indo-European conquest of the Harappan civilization, throwing India into religious turmoil out of which emerged Buddhism. Buddhistic principles became known to the west with Alexander's entrance into India. His conquest of "the world" began a spread of growing pantheonic irrelevance along with the emergence of many "mystery" religions that gave birth to Christianity. The turmoil within Christianity throughout Roman/ Byzantine times sparked a revolt within these one-world, one-god religions, a semblance of singularity was displayed by Buddhism, Christianity and Mohammedanism. This provided a foundation upon which the post-Roman, post-Han and post-Gupta civilizations survived their medievalism and advanced into the fifth phase. Now the state of religion at the beginning of phase seven has seen the ravages that scientific, cultural, economic and societal progress of phase five, and especially of the sixth phase, has had on these one-world, one-god religions. While there is public expressions of their veracity, a tacit realization of their growing irrelevance has gained a subconscious undercurrent throughout mankind's panessence. As a species mankind has begun a search for a new religious reality much like the Hellenistic period with its various "mystery" religions. These new mystery religions seek a true worldwide unity to which mankind can relate in order to advance into his future. They range from spiritual oneness of all humanity to the overriding of our worldly trappings by scientific fact. There is also the rise of "insignificantism" in testimonies of UFO sightings, extraterrestrial contacts and abductions; representing peoples of a far more advanced civilization to which we here on earth can aspire to achieve.

Even though religion evolved to allow mankind justifiable advancement into the unknown, his other developments weren't quite as ordered. Mankind's economic state during his transition from nature to ex-nature began with that of the immediate self and/or the clan. Though small entrepeneurships managed to survive through it all, the overall economy evolved through greater and greater sized units. The individual became a smaller and smaller part of this, especially when a single world-wide unitized economy dominates.

Capitalism served this system well through phase six. In fact, many times was political directions and social philosophy maneuvered to best take advantage of the benefits to be accrued from a laissez faire policy that garnered the most income for both entrepreneurs and governments. By the second half of phase six, however, signs that this long accepted system was running its course were becoming evident. Coupled with the increasing demands of a burgeoning population, the exploitation of nature to satisfy these demands was beginning to show negative results. Additionally, with scientific and technological advancement bringing to an end the labor intensiveness upon which the whole economic system depended, and economic revolution must occur.

Such a revolution does occur in two of the future scenarios described below. It is such a revolution that its apparent extremism constitutes an intrusive change of some magnitude: The old rules of work to earn an income in order to live will change. It will be instead a cooperative system in which work will still be done, but there will be an absence of money. Manufacturing and other production will be totally automated, utilizing a system in which everything is recycled. All goods and services provided by this system will be acquired by need, each individual aware that his presence in concert with all other individuals in the world-society/economy is part of the overall auto-mated production in which all share. This is not the Communism that characterized several countries during the Great Transition, for their populations were nowhere near a cognizance of the Panessence that this requires, nor were they part of a unified world economy that must exist before such a system can evolve.

Education's evolution began with a "hands on" inculcation so that each was thoroughly inured to living within the natural world. It ended with a system that imparts the complexity of a technological/scientific non-natural world. It ranged from a family ori-ented system, through one that was community standardized to a system of world-wide community orientation. At first distinct schools weren't needed as elder guided experience sufficed. During prehistoric lithic civilization, the complexities of some parts of civilization already had become such that apprenticeships were necessary. This because there were nascent industries that required more focused training—pottery, arms making, textile making, etc. Even as agriculture came into its own, replacing hunting-gathering, experience was still the primary means of education. Apprenticeships were still needed, especially now that there was far more technological and bureaucratic complexity in society for which specialized training was necessary. By the time lan-guage was being written and records began to be kept, those apprenticeships that trained for bureaucratic positions became schools in a real sense, though their curricula were limited. With the end of Rome, Han and Gupta, these schools became religious "academies" that concentrated more on scripture that the literature of government. Training in business and industry remained by apprenticeship.

As the Byzantine empire was nearing its end, some of these religious academies—and even some individuals—began a feverish campaign of salvaging and translating works of ancient authors. In this way Greek and Roman science, philosophy and literature was brought into Europe, sparking a widening interest in the world beyond scripture and fueling the rising European dynamic. This new knowledge could not be handled by the religiously oriented "academies", for the curiosity about the world beyond scripture that it spurred required a different approach. It had to be systematically organized—a situation that led to the birth of the modern university and provided a springboard for scientific and technological research.

By the Great Transition, the educational system—as a precursor to that beyond phase seven—had replaced almost all apprenticeship training. The dwindling number of apprenticeships that remained were in those labor intensive industries that were as of yet unautomated—mainly construction work. But even with this state of things, education was creating its own irrelevance: As technology continued its advance, spurring the growing cybernation of the physical aspect of civilization, educational training became more specialized as students were trained for narrower and narrower technological fields. When, far along in phase seven, the broad consensus of a world-wide society begins to emerge, things will happen to education: In the short term it will train people for their specialty within the economy. During this same short term it will be providing a broad picture—interconnecting the many specialties so that the individual will understand his place in a complex civilization.

The other function education will perform is preservation of the past. While the post-phase seven society will be of one race, one culture and in reality one ethnicity—it is essential that the rich history that preceded this time be preserved. Though the seven phases that marked mankind's progress into his post-seventh phase civilization seemed chaotic, it nevertheless provided fertile ground for a wide range of cultural development that gave the broadest range for consensus building. To lose all of this would indeed be tragic. For this cultural legacy mirrors mankind's rich societal evolution and presents a view of the various ways in which humanity organized his societies in relationship to their environments.

As has been outlined, society/civilization was a major player in humanity's seven phases of evolution. Unlike scientific advancement that rested on the accumulation of evidence, social development was at the whims of mankind's spirit, and so racked by consensus building conflicts. Oftentimes there were clashes among them. These conflicts continued through all seven phases beginning from where all were forced to live a certain way by the demands of nature. There were, of course, regional environmental differences that gave rise to the eventual differences in tribal attributes. These differences became important as populations grew requiring greater governmental organization that decreased their flexibility to adapt to changing conditions. Differences became intrusive change and seven phases of history became a record of mankind living through a period of being forced to change by economic demands and other pressures on his civilization. That Dark Age was a period of redefinition. Its overall character, one of turmoil—ie; continual readjustment to intrusive change—created instabilities that ranged from the individual, through families to whole nations. Aberrant behaviors were widely varied, many that were considered criminal. Some became crimes, others were no longer considered crimes. Politics ranged from obeisance to kings through democracy to anarchy.

After these seven phases of "Dark Age" evolution there emerged a redefined civilization completely unrelated to nature. The world-wide consensus that emerged through this readjustment period created a world-wide community/government with completely different standards of reference. The old standards that dictated society, economy, culture, philosophy, religion, etc are now gone.

Now there are new definitions; new parameters of normalcy or what is considered "natural". This means those terms that are used in describing mankind's many attributes have become based upon the new parameter of existence: A single language is used world-wide; the individual has become a state of mind, and not defined by outward physical appearance; the family—which went through a transition phase during the end of phase seven: Returning to its original purpose; that of preparing children for the future. Under whatever combination of adults this constituted—two of the same sex, opposite sex, different "races", single parent of either sex, or group family—the community interaction among them paved the way for children to accept the future. For those many communities were but a stepping-stone to the final world-wide community—those many communities superceded the raising of children by the singular family and were in turn superceded at the end of phase seven by the world-community in that function; government (except in one scenario described below) has become not much different than the many communities that make it up. In fact it is actually a supracommunity that embraces all of Earth. With the rapidity of information storage and retrieval—and the ease of access that all citizens have—all of the world has become local.

Cultural pursuits continue (except in two scenarios described below in which they become propaganda) for they are the glue that unites the human community: Art, music, history and literature retain their agelessness; still extolling mankind's virtues, reminding us of his evils, displaying his emotions, enumerating his philosophies, justifying his religions, mirroring his imagination, recording his science—an eclectic collection that has been mankind's diary throughout all seven phases of the Dark Age. Yet the past is not forgotten; how else but by preserving and knowing this cultural legacy would we truly comprehend the nature of mankind?

Despite the continuation of cultural mechanisms for eliciting emotional empathy, the post-seventh phase world is one where true understanding of mankind's historical emotional richness is little understood. For by moving himself from a being **of** nature to one **without** nature, he has eliminated those conditions for which the emotions were developed—except in the first scenario below. With the absence of disease, aberrant behavior and an intrusive level of crime, there no longer exists conditions that call up various emotional states. This future society displays a certain stoicism a measure of "matter of factness"—that recalls the acceptance of occurrences that characterized human society before he began his evolutionary transition to being separate from nature. Then, occurrences considered criminal or tragic or sad, etc, before the long Dark Age were accepted as fate, part of the give and take of living within nature. In post-seventh phase society, these no longer exist and so any need for emotional conditionalizing no longer exists. Emotionalism is replaced by knowledge of the full range of human existence, mainly his psychological intertwinings for which society has become structured.

Perhaps one of the greatest changes through which mankind's society evolved is the acceptance that individualism can exist within a community. Any community or communal organization—government, tribe, religion, etc—are actual expressions of distrust. They provide mechanisms that enables the individual to place his faith knowing (trusting) that others who also do so are of the same mind or timbre and can therefore be trusted. When humans were of nature, every region had requirements for survival within their environments. This meant everyone within that region pretty much had to follow the same lifestyle—evolved over time—to assure their survival. In this prehistoric period of early hunter-gatherer days, when mankind relied solely on nature, trust was more of a faith because all had to live by nature's rules and accept her whims. As mankind evolved on his period of change between of to separate from nature, he brought this need for unity with him. Since spirit took over establishing reason for being, shared ambience with nature was replaced by unity of opinion, spirit's only mechanism for guidance. So there was a long period of battle over which unity of opinion was acceptable. There was religious unity. There was governmental unity. Sometimes they were separate, sometimes combined. Often one was the reason for justifying the other.

At times throughout mankind's history, there have been thinkers expressing the possibility of human fulfillment by allowing greater freedom for the individual. There have even been times when it was tried: The period of Greek democracy, the period of Roman republicanism before Caesar, the widespread individualism of Hindu belief that led one wag to remark "there are as many Hindu religions as there are Hindus", to name a few. These, and many lesser examples, were still constrained by the needs of security in conformity to demand some measure of unified belief or standardized social activity.

Toward the end of phase five as Europe was entering that period known as the Renaissance, and especially during phase six—the Great Transition—realization that a unity of belief or standardized social activity was unnecessary for a benign society to exist was capturing the minds of an increasing number of people. Movements began to abolish slavery, for religious tolerance, for racial tolerance, for ending censorship, reducing trade sanctions, easing rigid currency rules, and changing or abolishing many other rules and practices. These were left over from those perceived days of insecurity when unanimity was thought to be the only way to assure security. And perhaps it was, for despite the world opening effect of the printing press, the number of people exposed was limited. Even into the Industrial Revolution, great numbers of people remained parochial in their concept of the world around them. For communication was still limited and relatively slow.

But the paramount effect the Great Transition had on mankind was that it prepared him for beginning to form into a global village—of one religion, one language, one "ethnicity", one set of social mores, one cultural "standard" or set of standards. These "ones", however, are not monolithic, for they are more conceptual than physical since individualism can exist within them: They represent a consensus of any number of attributes among individuals. In the post-seventh phase society, the third one described below, the vitality of individual minds will not be lost though they work within their societal consensus. It was this struggle of individualism versus society that underlaid the tumultuousness marking mankind's evolution through history.

These conflicts among religion, economics, education, society, culture and scientific advancement seemed to be never ending, producing a continuous imposition of change upon a being constantly seeking stasis and individual fulfillment. We have traced these changes and their reaction to them through seven phases of time that mark the evolutionary interval that is history. We have seen that it is an interval between existing with nature to the state of being completely separate from it. It was the Great Transition—phase six—that was the era that mankind sealed his fate to be eventually separated completely from nature. During this period he devised systems that were faster—transportation, communication, disease fighting, etc— than nature's systems. As these new processes advanced, nature had to give way, for they did not lend themselves to natural flows. Their rapid development and sophistication only widened the distance from which mankind had separated from nature. Being separate from nature, as we have seen, maximizes cellular security, for only that way is the cell free from predators. After the end of the Great Transition and well into the last phase, the seventh, this status of being separated from nature as much as possible—maximizing cellular security (at least those of the human organization)—was well underway. Complicating this progress was human development that went from the generalism of hunter-gatherer days to managed hyper-specialization of the modern scientific/technological civilization. As if mocking nature—where each species has its specialized niche and are all "managed" by Nature's Ways—mankind was compartmentalizing himself, to be managed by others of his species who were deemed capable of doing so. This hyper-specialization went far beyond tasks, but emerged as "ethnic" identities, various cults—religious and otherwise, racial divisions, clubs, parties and other group associations lacking the "big picture" view required of the dawning world-nation. The seventh phase can be characterized as a second medieval period. More properly a Neo-Medieval era, in which reaction to the one-worldism of the

Great Transition drove mankind to withdraw into small familiar units (neighborhoods, ethnicities, groups, parties, etc) from which to more easily consider and try to understand the new state of affairs. Just as with the collapse of Rome, Han and Gupta where local orientation became commonplace (medievalism) and human spirit had to consider the world's state. So it is throughout the seventh phase; even though there are powerful forces pushing to maintain the old forms, the stridency of their proponents belie the subconscious awareness of their increasing irrelevance. Thus the seventh phase will usher in the end of history as Earth will possibly become one government, one community, one economy—a world-nation.

Using the word "possibly" indicates that this future may not be what's in store. For mankind has a choice between two possible futures, and it is up to the direction taken by his consensus as to which he chooses. The first is to descend into tribalism, or at least a never ending continuation of history, with all of its ethnic and religious conflicts, social and moral conflicts, economic and regular warfare and continuing environmental and species destruction. For if in the course of the seventh phase, mankind decides not to comply with a worldwide consensus on what constitutes a family, on racial attitudes, on morality, on what religion will dominate, what language will be spoken, and a myriad of other subjects (including such seemingly inconsequential ones such as the standard of beauty, appropriate dress, animal rights, table manners, etc), he will have thwarted the aim of his evolution, and that is to provide cell security. He will have abandoned recovering his Panessence, that interspiritual connection enjoyed by all other species, given up so long ago during his hunter-gatherer days. The times will be tumultuous, though as in all tumultuous times, art, music and literature will flourish. Only for awhile, however, for without growth, expansion and development but rather the inevitable exhaustion from constant conflict will even snuff out these expressions of the human spirit. It will be a triumph for the bourgeoisie, for they will have gained control over society and government. Their anti-government philosophy, misconstrued as "conservatism", will only exacerbate neo-tribalism, driving humanity into the direst of straits. The European dynamic that brought mankind to such accomplishment will become enervated. Mankind will not have reacquired his Panessence which is necessary in order to rise out of his Dark Age. It may mean the eventual end of the human species.

Option two is of course to continue his evolution so that cell security is attained. Throughout phase seven, the earth's population broke up into smaller and smaller governmental units: The ubiquitousness of information availability and rapidity of its transmission brought about a decline of the effectiveness of many of the organizations that served mankind throughout his long dark age; religious establishments, nation-states and cultural standards that served these ends. World orientation, however, at first does not seem to serve these characteristics, so new standards are searched for. This can only be done from the framework of interconnected parochial units. A search for meaning is begun, for those that served (and were fought over) through seven phases are now irrelevant.

This was the chaotic nature of the seventh phase: There was a gradual evolution of consensi that included greater numbers of groups. These consensi then began to coalesce into a world-wide consensus. By the end of the phase, this world consensus had emerged—and along with it a World Nation. Finally, the world state that had underwritten all history had finally been achieved. But its characteristics are not what was envisioned at the end of the Great Transition. Now there is unanimity of social consciousness; society has become unified into a single "community" or world society. The divergencies of spirit that so enlivened history have been attenuated. The emotionalism that drove those divergent spirits has been abandoned. From the perspective at the end of the Great Transition this apparent loss of individual freedom, of localized control of one's destiny, indeed even of the old governmental forms, seems opprobrious. But evolution of a world-nation can only occur from a fully interconnected (a ubiquitous information network) world-wide cooperative of localized areas. As each adjusts to better meld with others in an ever widening circle, the consensus slowly develops. As this occurs, the old governmental forms, the borders of the nation-states and the cultural attributes that were local or regional in nature become irrelevant. The technological/informational state of the world-nation can provide total freedom within its new parameters: Mankind will have adapted to a world-wide consensus. All will have been judged, all will have been reformed. History will be seen as having been a record of parochialism as the world has become one community, one government, one economy—one culture. But even at this point there are two choices as to what the shape of this world-wide community will be. One is the complete opposite of that just described. In this scenario, mankind acquiesces in submission to a world-wide government of complete control over all facets of every individual's life. He will have become a population of automatons living in an extremely structured society. This ant-like civilization **does** provide complete safety and security for each individual and, therefore, achieves that long sought cellular security. But at what price? Humankind becomes a population of mindless individuals of the mass, world-wide mind. There are several classes within society; government, the bureaucracy, held by the highest class, is of course the manager, raising psychology to a fine art, manipulating even the Panessence. But it is a structured Panessence, without any latitude for allowing any expression of humanity's irrepressible Spirit with its penchant for inventiveness and creativity. This is a civilization of hyperspecialization in which any expression of the spirit is strictly controlled. The highly specialized class—or "technocrats"—are the specialty educated, manning the computers that control the great automated economic system. The third class or "underclass"—comprises the uneducated; those who perform what remaining tasks there are requiring manual labor. Thus cultural expression and other forms of "free" thought become hollow statements that serve society's "meaning" or purpose—tiredly overdrawn through endless tautological repetitions of the benefits of collective security. The European dynamic disappears as mankind settles into an ant-like stasis—a constancy that results in a society that maintains itself by sheer force of the purpose only of maintaining itself. As this society concentrates all of its energy on maintaining the status-quo, and having lost the drive of the European dynamic, it becomes monotonous. Without any drive for expansion and development, it becomes like other species who are limited to their environmental niche: It must hope that conditions remain unchanged for its existence. The dynamism that made mankind stand out among all of Earth's species is gone. Any expansion or exploration is machine-like, the emotionalism that Spirit brought to human affairs is gone. Though complete cellular security has been achieved, eventually complete enervation sets in and the end of the species will soon result.

For the second choice, mankind opts to retain his individualism, and his sense of individual freedom. This freedom, however, is not social or physical, but is individual freedom of one's mental existence. Physical or social individuality has been subserviated to a quasi-monarchial world-state—a sort of "corporate community" in which there are no distinct "boundaries" among the governmental, economic and social functions of society.

Religion will have been the first to evolve, for it must lead and therefore is of necessity ecumenical. All of the old religions will be relegated to the library's mythology section as the new is a whole world religion—having prepared mankind to accept and live within the nation-world and move beyond. No longer does religion strive to address one's relationship to the world, and attempt to influence how the world treats the individual. Religion now addresses the soul's identity within the mass society of the world-nation. Psychology has taken over religion's previous function, for it, bolstered by science, provides explanations and reasons for the world-nation/individual relationship. Psychology provides meaning tieing **all** together. It is the premier science of the future. It is the new religion that leads the way for mankind to accept his future, but with a religious adjunct: Of all that religion encompassed throughout history, it now schools the soul with but one rule. This is of course the "Golden Rule"—treat all as you would have all treat you—which could be called the basic tenet of the world-nation.

The nature of society is thus defined—"all" includes air, earth, water, flora and fauna: A truly ecumenical religious state cannot exclude any part of the universe, or else it is restrictively parochial.

Education encompasses the global nature of economic, social and political thinking as well as technical mission. It represents the return of the generalist, that all must be if the world-nation is to function in a satisfactory way. As Woodrow Wilson wrote in his speech of July, 1893: The aim of education is to give the average citizen a comprehension of his own times and the forces at work in them. "Of all things that a [school] should do...the most important is to put [the citizen] in possession of the material for a systematic criticism of life." Inotherwords, the student should be educated to become both a critic and an interpreter of life. The members of humankind thus become true individuals; a people of knowledge. All will have been given a liberal education (generalism) yet have stressed a specialty—necessary to fit into the new economic organization of the world-nation. The two are different and education must reflect this. As Mr Wilson continued: Literature and history do not lend themselves to being taught by scientific method. People should "know the probabilities of failure and success, can separate the tendencies which are permanent from the tendencies which are of the moment merely." Inotherwords, each individual accepts self-responsibility. This means in the society of the future, each will be conversant with both the Panessence and the many facets that make up society which will be as second nature as an autonomic reaction.

Government, too, struggles with meaning. Its predilection to micromanage citizen's lives gives way as it is reduced to serving only several functions: One of these is the maintenance of economic stability. But this role will become less important as the world-nation becomes a community wherein economic fluctuations don't bring the possibility of severe impacts as they did in the days of the nation-states. The antagonisms that characterized settling economic problems among nation-states attenuates to solving the same problems **within** a nation-state, only now on a world-wide basis. Eventually, as the seventh phase fades into the past, even these differences will disappear. Communication and information retrieval will become so convenient that a world-wide economy will function like that of a household. Even the money value parameters of "velocity" and "trade balance" will have no meaning. The necessity of work and the stigma of welfare and poverty, will no longer be factors in the health of the economy. Even "economy" as a subject will disappear as it too will become meaningless, for existence will be quite different in the wholly integrated society of the post-phase seven world.

Another function of government is the maintenance of educational constancy and quality. Even though a world-wide society eventually loses all disruption by intrusive change, knowledge of mankind's tumultuous past must not be lost. Even though we may look back on that long record of warfare, slavery, exploitation, holocausts and destruction and say "good riddance" they nevertheless defined mankind. Though they occurred, there had always been, by some, a constant push to end these deterrents to human advancement. How mankind reacted, how his consensus struggled to find a way to prevent these from happening again is what defined humanity. In the post-phase seven world-nation that is without intrusive change and therefore never to see these occurrences again, the desire to forget the past must not be satisfied. To do so would enervate society for, as Woodrow Wilson wrote, we must know of civilization its "elements which run centuries deep into the history of nations": Without a grounding in history, philosophy and literature [we] could know only the technical rules "which must for [us] be rules dead, inflexible, final"; it is education's duty to make sure this doesn't happen. We would be, as Mr Wilson continued, "in danger to lose our identity and become infantile in every generation. [Individuals] of the world in the best sense are what they ought to be: [Those] who would not be taken in by the world's shows, or misled by fashion or popularity." Thus education, as a government function, must assure each citizen of the world-nation is conversant with mankind's cultural past. By doing so, descent into an ant-like society is prevented, and venturing into the future is done from a rich foundation built by a consensus that has made comprehension of mankind's past part of his Panessence.

The function of government then is that of an administrator. Since the post-phase seven civilization is one of specialists within a generalized world, government is more a bureaucratic function that a director: The phase-era competition and adversarial posturings among the various parts of society have become one system—unitized by the demands of the ever-growing awareness of their inter-relationships—and now needing only an operational organization to keep it going. The aim for humans, of course, as has been the aim all through history, is to maximize personal fulfillment. Individualism becomes of the mind and not physical (internal and not external) as Spirit has abandoned Nature based (religious) concepts of reason for being. The mass of humanity becomes "being", a community—a species of interconnected souls: Mankind is again ruled by the Panessence. Cellular security has thus been achieved as humanity is reacquainted with his soul, living in concert not unlike the ancient cellular societies from which he ultimately evolved. But these relationships have been tempered by Spirit, that for the first time in Earth's life has seen the rise of a being capable of exercising control over those forces that threaten cellular security. Ultimately, this has effected the course followed through mankind's phase-era, or "Dark Age", producing his post-phase society.

The shape of this society will be determined by the state of the final world-wide consensus. Mankind is no longer supreme, being now completely ex-Natura. His world-nation can only exist separate from nature only by its allowance to be without nature's interference. Human cell security is thus achieved by this new existence—for to be in any way socially or physically related to nature is to be subject to its diseases, genetic alterations, physical and psychological harm: Utilization of other species in the development of medicines and other chemicals to escape these natural occurrences only maintains the chance of being affected by them. The same happens when physically "out enjoying" nature. Also to use nature for adventure, whether hunting, camping, hiking, soaring, sailing, etc, is to similarly be exposed to her dangers. Perhaps the most difficult to change will be the use of nature for food. As long as mankind is dependent upon natural processes for sustenance, he will always be subject to nature's vicissitudes. In this society, mankind has learned that he obtains the freedom of cellular security only by being completely separated from nature. Throughout his long dark age, he struggled to dominate, to change and to control nature, but doing so only drew him deeper into the complexities of having to submit to "Nature's Ways". This only frustrated his attempts to be free of the consequences of nature's machinations. But now he has learned to leave nature alone—to allow those other species that share the earth with him to live as they wish, while mankind only dominates a minimal area. This means that the physical shape of our future civilization is one of extreme compactness; no longer is spreading out all over the surface of the Earth equated with great prowess. Now it is the non-natural civilization that expands with the mind—leaving nature alone—that will carry mankind into his future.

So what we can hope our eventual society will be like is one that includes all of this last. But the shape of this society is completely alien to our present concepts. Family, neighborhood, community are no longer separate as discernable or distinct sectors. They have become blended into one world-wide society that raises children, educates us, maintains the economy and assures cultural links with our past as well as provides for future cultural development. Our external, or physical, lives will no longer be under individual control, but managed by society—since "government" as we know it will no longer exist—controlling birth rates, our health, where and how we live, etc. Work and employment will also be a part of our functioning society—since labor, employment and economics as we know them will no longer exist. Inotherwords, the human species will become not unlike his own makeup as a well-run mechanism of highly organized cells. Only now it will be a well-run mechanism of highly organized humans which, just like the organization of cells, is interconnected by and sharing through the Panessence.

Mankind will once again have returned to the singular species he began as so long ago. Whereas then the laws of nature controlled his population and all aspects of his existence, now the social laws of his nation-world community perform these functions. It is as if the long Dark Age had been a record of ever increasing and multiplying ripples upon the pond of mankind's existence. The greatest of all cycles has been completed, from unity to chaos to unity. Now in the post seventh phase era, mankind has returned to his species unity. The status-quo and stasis he so avidly sought has finally arrived, though, now completely separated from nature, it is society run, not nature as before.

EPILOGUE

Crises are not new to human society. In fact, mankind has never been crisis-free for any substantial period of time. As we have seen, the intrusive change brought by these crises, and the reaction to them, reformed societies to better adjust to the newer parameters. Many times, however, a few societies have "jumped the gun" so to speak, attempted to utilize their new conceptualization to conteract the intrusive change in an effort, it not to stop it, to move it in a certain direction. Thus a sort of self-inflicted intrusive change was inaugurated either by laws being handed down or by the rise of popular movements. Not only was the reaction to intrusive change sometimes countered, but internal forces, themselves a sort of self-made self-inflicted intrusive change, were also countered.

In early Sumeria the Church, that managed grain storage and distribution, began to take advantage of this position to gain control of society. So kings assumed greater powers in order to protect the lower classes from being victimized by this. Kings such as Sargon, Naram-Sin and Hammurabi decreed laws to establish the relationships among peoples and between groups. When the Bronze Age transformed into the Iron Age, industrialization began to create entrepreneurs that had an economic power on par with the political power of the landed gentry. These two, termed the bourgoisie in this book, exercised their assumed rights over society. This caused more of a reaction by the monarch, both to protect the lower classes and to save his own skin from designs of the landed gentry—oligarchs—on his position: It was birth of the Divine Right of Kings, for who could contest a leader chosen by God?

The Iron Age brought to the eyes of humanity a far more complex world. As we have seen, this gave the rise to the One God One World religions. Spurred by the strength of the percieved unanimity of these religions, great bourgoisie headed trading empires appeared. These corporate hegemonies (such as the Hanseatic League) began to assume the right to dictate various policies to the governments with which they dealt. This was in their own self interests—to preserve their markets and economic viability. But it didn't necessarily serve the interest of the governments involved, and soon actions—from laws to warfare—was taken by governments to restrain these organizations. In many cases governments created their own trading companies (such as the British and Dutch East India Companies) to counter private companies and maintain control of both trade and international relations.

Even religion suffered from its own action-reaction problems. When the Roman church assumed governmental duties in central and western Europe after the fall of Rome, it began a long trend of itself becoming a great corporation of sorts. It went through the throes of interpretation that the other religions went through, but by the late middle ages it had become insufferably unyielding in its assumed right of control over society and its rulers (after all, kings ruled by "Divine Right" and who but the pope decided that?) This gave rise to a reaction we call the rise of Protestantism. Eventually Protestantism itself became as insufferable as the Roman Church—especially the conflicts from not only Protestant—Catholic battles but also from battles among various Protestant sects. Looking for a little more stability, people began longing for a return to some kind of "order"; this gave rise to the counter reformation, a return to acceptance of Catholicism and its schools. And for those who wanted to be free of these religious conflicts, the United States Constitution was a watershed document that imposed a wall separating church and state.

With the dawn of the Industrial Revolution, the bourgoisie finally came into their own, gaining far greater power than the landed gentry ever had. Labor was plentiful, cheap and was utilized just like any other commodity. The reaction to this was slow but meaningful. Marx gave birth to the concept of Communism wherin the workers gain control of the bourgoisie—the modern day exploitive oligarchs. More significant was the rise of unions, as workers themselves struggled to make their lives better by forcing industrialists to treat them as human beings.

The French Revolution marked the end of the Divine Rights of kings (except in Japan) and WWI marked the end of free reign by the landed gentry. Between the two saw an incredible rise of the new industrial oligarchs (Theodore Roosevelt's "wealthy criminal class"). Their rise, and the end of WWI with the Russian revolution was the rise of Communism as an influential force greater than that of unionism. By the end of WWII, Communist hegemony was being countered by a new industrial militarism—Eisenhower's Military-Industrial complex. Toward the end of phase six, even as the Communist hegemony collapsed, society was being transformed into a corporate state as computerization and globalization enabled entrepreneurships to keep way ahead of their governments. In fact they almost became governments unto themselves. Just as in ancient Sumeria, governments struggled to gain control in order to—if not end, at least attenuate—abuses by the industrial behemoths upon the citizens they served. In many cases, especially in the United States, socialist minded people were appointed to various positions in government. This was not in an effort to change society into a socialist system, but it was an extreme shot seen as the only way to counter the growing business hegemony in hopes of arriving at a medial position.

This process will continue early in the seventh phase. It won't be confined to a few countries but will be world wide as humanity will see the emergence of a world corporate state. Actually this corporatization is necessary for future development: The world well be regionalized and then finally unified into a somewhat efficient corporate and economic whole because individually minded governments who are unwilling to defer to the UN are unable to do this. This corporate world, however, will eventually become stale (just as did the early trading empires and religious hegemonies) and there will be a groundswell of a socialist reaction. This will spark a resurgence of government not wishing to see economic vitality sapped by socialism. The rise of world socialist reaction to corporate hegemony will foster the rise of a true world government.

There have been other forced internal intrusive change that has not contributed to humanity's historical development. Fueled by moral stands and the inabilituy to be flexible, they have been detrimental and in fact had or could have the capacity of destroying the very society they were designed to save. Most notable were Prohibition and the War of Drugs in the United States. The former produced such a rise of lawlessness, police corruption and Draconian laws that the very fabric of constitutional society was threatened with destruction. It was only saved by the repeal of Prohibition (and the bombing of Pearl Harbor) and government regulation of the liquor industry. The War on Drugs, conceived in haste but far more difficult to attenuate because it was global in scope, was even greater in its capability to destroy the society it was striving to save. Laws were passed that seriously eroded property rights (asset forfeiture, etc) and judicial humanity/compassion (mandatory sentencing, etc). Drug use became a crime whose punishment was more severe that that of a murderer, pedophile or drunk driver who kills someone while under the influence—prisons became a growth industry from the needs to long-term house growing numbers of non-violent inmates who had been drug users.

The War on Drugs fractionated society producing two major divisions polarizing the people to where continuation of society becomes ever more difficult: Those who support a more authoritarian society in order to control its problems and those who support drug management that doesn't overly tax the taxpayer as does the former. This latter group is divided into two factions: Those who support a Swiss style drug management program; those who support rehabilitation—much like what came out of alcohol policy—and those who call for the outright legalization (and taxation) of drugs. It wont be the first civilization faced by the danger of being weakened by such internecine strife.

TOWARD THE FUTURE

Slave to no sect,
who takes no private road,
But looks through Nature
up to Nature's God.

Alexander Pope

The key for mankind to achieve the one-world community necessary for him to continue evolution and advancement into the future is the mythology of religion. Without a new mythology that addresses this future in terms of that future, advancement is impossible. Since the mythology of religion programs human minds in relation to all other things, it is thus necessary for the new programming to be receptive to the new relationships that will be normal in the future. This means the very thought processes humans utilize in assessing information and determining utility and value must be changed. As the mythology of religion plays a large part in dictating the path of thought processes, only it can manage the necessary changes in these processes.

Since the future is unknown, only a new mythology that can accommodate the unforseen can allow humanity to handle the future as it unfolds. As we have seen, these mythologies—expressed as religious beliefs—have had to change because their ability to accommodate future conditions were limited. This was because the mythologies had to be created and directed by one or more gods. While they were mythological, they could be construed as real, enabling various societies to achieve a commonality within the mythology. These gods were Earth-bound gods born of regional characteristics. Their dictates and tenets of behavior, morals, etc., attempted to have a world view. Nevertheless, they retained their regional characteristics. Furthermore, the very world they tried to address became much larger and more complex than the founders foresaw. Their mythologies became trite as the world grew beyond their limitations. Their religions—like Ptolemy's universe—had to be rewritten, reconstrued and apologetically adjusted to better fit the increasing variations of society as more of the world came into view. Now as mankind is being forced to accept that his "world view" must actually **be** a World View, these old religions, so accretioned with modifications, have slowly lost their efficacy. And they have lost their relevance.

For mankind to enter his future, he must understand God is larger than the Earth, encompassing **all** of the universe. His breath, sign of the presence of a "living" god, is evidenced by the life-like pulsations occurring throughout this infinite universe. God's law is thus those rules that dictate existence—whether a galaxy, a system, a planet or one member of a species interacting with others—in this universe. Our Earth is merely a microcosm in this infinite vastness. Realization of this state brings to bear the manifestation of God.

Soul now gains its true state, embracing the interconnectivity of existence—of all life—in all of its forms as it struggles to succeed within the laws of existence. This struggle is shared by all members of the universe, and its manifestation is fairly similar. For those "inanimate" members, all obey the laws of physics, and are subject to any vicissitudes that the laws of probability may bring to bear. They are subject to gravity, collision, radiation, surface irregularity, physical form and—our Earth is an example—the physical strains from plate tectonics, rotational wobble, etc. Those considered "animate" not only share obeisance to the laws of physics, but also to those laws of existence we have encompassed with Darwinian parameters: Animate beings are subject to the many faces of competition and the demands of adaptation, to the push of mutation and to changes in their physical environment. So now the soul is attuned to not only the symphony of our universe, but to the great unity of existence shared by all animate beings. While form may differ—ie, beings from other worlds—they have the same likes, dislikes and needs for satisfaction. All like to be adequately nourished, comfortable in their existence and free from adversity. Even though individuals may differ as to outlook, opinions, method of quest—basically the way they associate experiences—they enter the ending of our dark age with this understanding of the universality of existence and how soul is the key that ties all existence together.

Spirit remains unchanged as humankind moves beyond his dark age. It is redirected, however, for now with knowledge of soul—which before was only guessed at—humans no longer must waste their spirit energy in a quest to establish meaning. Meaning is now known in the great scheme of the universe. Their orientation and relationships among all other members of the universe is known. Spirit's energy thus propels humanity in a new quest for learning, a quest of exploration.

Humankind's new mythology will be that state of existence in which he has found salvation and been redeemed. This mythology must be expressed as a new religion onto which each individual can grasp to be carried into the future. Thus humankind finds salvation in the redemption of coming to know his true self in post-dark age existence. Salvation is that state of knowledge in which its presence is not so much a discovery as it is innate. It is, inotherwords, beyond understanding for it is a condition that no longer needs to be "learned" or "understood". The innateness of salvation means that the very fiber of each individual throbs with the rhythms of the universe. And thus with humankind in concert with the universe he achieves his redemption. His redemption is the achievement—the innate or subconscious knowledge and understanding—of the "universality" of mankind. Humankind, like all other life forms, is redeemed in that the death of individuals is superseded by continuance of Soul through the generations.

With the new consciousness Phase Seven comes to an end. Human civilization, now a world-wide community, will have a new "set", one that is naturally acquiesced to by all. A new set no longer encumbered by the local and/or regional differences that plagued humanity throughout his Dark Age. Only with a world-wide community of universal customs, laws, morals, language and various other standards to which each readily acquiesces, will mankind be able to reach into his future.

Perhaps one of the most important relationships that the new religion will impact is the necessity for a new economic order. Up through the fifth phase, all relationships each person has had with his economic climate have been resultants of the old earth-bound regional religions: A person's worth is gauged by his performance, his capability of producing for the economic good of society at large and his ability to economically "fend for himself". The new religion must now recast this perception of each person's worth in a completely different light: As technology, along with its cybernetic sophistication, along with chemical, biological and genetic sophistication, virtually eliminate both the natural challenges to existence and the need for a "work ethic" to evaluate one's status; human worth becomes measured in more philosophical terms. A new currency evolves in which society's transactions are not exchanges of physical value, but are exchanges within a single body of which each citizen is a part. The economy becomes no longer definable as each individual is related to it as each cell is related to the body of which it is a part. As in the body, each cell is provided for by its need—so in the new economy is each citizen sustained. In the body there are white blood cells that fight infection, and other cells that repair damage. So too in the new economy, there are care-takers who maintain the cybernetic production mechanism of the system. In the new economy of the future, **all** is manufactured. Even food, for to rely of natural—farm—production is to inject the uncertainty of nature into a wholly organized and regulated system. This means there is total recycling, with very little additions of raw material from the outside. Any raw materials (minerals, fluids, organic compounds, etc.) that are added are thoroughly sterilized before they are allowed in the system.

As in the body, regardless of "status", every cell partakes equally in its maintenance. There is a hierarchy—in the body of cells, in the future economy of persons—that only comes into play if the existence of the body/economy is threatened: An order of sacrifice comes into place while the threat is combatted in order to be able to rebuild when, and if, the threat is defeated.

As the new economy comes into full swing, it will automatically herald the complete unification of humankind into a single society—a global community intimately interlinked through a benevolent cybernetic mechanism. In this society, moral codes will also have been dramatically changed: No longer will individual directions be controlled by these ancient codes that were born of surviving the battle with nature or with hostile neighbors. Any formal type of moral code or tacit societal agreements that have been the basis for law and community "norms", have been replaced by a process of "in context" analysis. That is, rigid codes have been replaced by understanding of the psychological conditions under which each individual labors. Though by the final stages of mankind's arrival at his world society completely separate from nature, each person will be part of the whole. All of this world-wide society will function as a single mechanism—the need for moral codes or parameters will have become moot. Humanity will have become that of its dream, to live harmoniously as "one"—one mind, one language, one ambition and one dream.

But what of the irrepressible spirit of the individual? To suppress this is to destroy the very essence of mankind. And what of the European dynamic, that "force" of his spirit that brought a continuous stream of intrusive change down upon humanity's head forcing him to develop into his future? Mankind is now separate from Nature, being a new part of the universe no longer with any affiliation with the Earth from which he sprung. His global economy has matured and soon even the present becomes stale with the future again uncertain.

Now will the European dynamic come into play, now as the genius of the total human spirit, and mankind will go into space—his last great frontier. The human species will begin a new vast order of existence. It will include a new vast economy of almost unlimited expansion opportunities. His expansion will struggle for the far reaches of the universe already imagined by his new mythology. This will begin a new cycle, for he will be separating from Earth, just as before when he separated from Nature. As a single society/community reaching beyond the planet of his birth, humankind truly becomes a child of the universe. His existence will be assured, and he will live on long after the Sun has gone.